Richard has structured his book from an insiders ~~of what it takes, step-by-step, to achieve your go~~ roadmap to success from a true master of the cra

> — Toby M. Bronson, *Pirates of the Caribbean, The Aviator, Deadwood*

The information in this book is both true and valuable, and anyone who reads it has access to years of the kind of mentorship that has largely vanished from our industry.

> — Edward Marks, President, Western Costume Company

Costume Design 101 is an invaluable resource for any writer, director or producer who wants to create and run TV shows or produce their own movies. Why? Because it's not just about costumes — it's about *how to run the actual department* — which means it should be required reading for anyone hoping to oversee a full-scale TV or film production.

> — Chad Gervich, TV Writer/Producer (*Smash Cuts, Speeders, Reality Binge, Foody Call*) and author of *Small Screen, Big Picture: A Writer's Guide to the TV Business*

Dreaming of a fascinating and lucrative career in costume design for film and television? *Costume Design 101* is filled with real-world information and insights, written by an experienced, professional costume designer. This detailed book is the only one you'll need to succeed in the current realm of theatrical costume design! You'll experience the fun of learning about designing wardrobes for films and TV shows, as well as the practical elements of this creative profession: how to break down a script for wardrobe requirements; budgeting; the various ways to provide the costumes; plus working well with actors, directors, film crews, and producers. No detail or aspect of costume design is omitted. Let Richard La Motte be your mentor!

> — Elizabeth English, Founder & Executive Director
> Moondance International Film Festival

The cross-referencing of material throughout the book makes it easy to understand how all the different bits of information relate to each other. The explanation of color theory and lighting is clear and concise — probably one of the most comprehensive I've come across. Bottom line, reading this book will give anyone an advantage when doing his or her first show.

> — Maria Lorenzana Costume Designer/Instructor, Columbia College

What an absolute joy it is to know that the true art of costume design and filmmaking is being conveyed to everyone who reads this book. It is an absolute privilege to have this wealth of information compiled for everyone to enjoy. Thank you, Richard, for sharing your valuable knowledge with all of us who aspire to be great.

> — Diana Foster, President of American Costume Company

This book should become the bible for other costume designers. It's clear and comprehensive.

> — Erica Phillips, Costume Designer, *The Perfect Storm, Air Force One, Outbreak, The General's Daughter*

Richard La Motte has brought every day of his 40 years of experience to the page in *Costume Design 101*, and it shows. A more comprehensive, thoroughly practical guide to running a wardrobe department would be hard to find.

— Robert Grant, SCI-FI-LONDON

Richard loves his craft and it shows in every line. He has given us a comprehensive, step-by-step analysis of the costume designer's work. Of great value to both the interested amateur and the budding professional.

— John Bloomfield, Costume Designer, *The Mummy*, *Waterworld*, *The Scorpion King*

Richard unlocks the door to costume design in a way that makes complex concepts easy to understand. I wish I had a book like this when I was starting out.

— Robert Turturice, Costume Designer, *Batman and Robin*, *The Flintstones in Viva Rock Vegas*

An accurate and insightful look at the behind-the-scenes requirements... for anyone interested in a career in wardrobe. An entertaining read for the general public, as well as professionals.

— Molly Harris Campbell, Costume Designer, *Beverly Hills 90210*, *The X-Files*

Because costuming can 'make or break' a production, it's essential that those in the wardrobe department are organized, efficient, and knowledgeable, and La Motte does a great job explaining how to achieve that. La Motte's extensive knowledge and his passion and enthusiasm for his work clearly shine throughout the book, and it's almost impossible to not catch it.

— Kari Ann Morgan, Book Editor, *Microfilmmaker* Magazine

From first stitch to final seam, *Costume Design 101* is an incredible book that offers powerful insights into the role of a costumer for film and television. The book is a must have for anyone serious about working in Costume Design, and covers everything from getting started in the business to sketching your costume designs for a director. Complete with illustrations and tons of helpful pointers for the newcomers to the business, *Costume Design 101* was an absolute joy to read.

— Mark Sickle, Managing Editor, *Independent Source* Magazine

Never having been involved in high-budget film production, I didn't know how much effort went into costume design! In *Costume Design 101*, author Richard La Motte, with over 20 years of experience, walks the reader through the business of costume design involved in production. The book offers guidance on getting hired (by designing perfect portfolios and resumes) all the way to working in the field. Including over 30 costume illustrations, you'll find yourself entranced by the world of costume design. And like me, you may have found yourself a new profession!

— Amanda Porter, Associate Editor, *School Video News*

COSTUME DESIGN 101
THE BUSINESS AND ART OF CREATING COSTUMES FOR FILM AND TELEVISION

SECOND EDITION

Richard La Motte

Published by Michael Wiese Productions
3940 Laurel Canyon Blvd. # 1111
Studio City, CA 91604
tel. 818.379.8799
fax 818.986.3408
mw@mwp.com
www.mwp.com

Cover Design: MWP
Book Layout: Gina Mansfield Design
Editor: Art Insana

Printed by McNaughton & Gunn, Inc., Saline, Michigan
Manufactured in the United States of America

Library of Congress Cataloging-in-Publication Data

La Motte, Richard, 1943-
 Costume design 101 / by Richard La Motte. -- 2nd ed.
     p. cm.
 ISBN 978-1-932907-69-8
 1. Costume. 2. Costume design. I. Title.
 PN1995.9.C56L32 2010
 791.4302'6--dc22

                                        2009029886

TABLE OF CONTENTS

FOREWORD
TO THE
SECOND EDITION

Originally, the publisher told me that the biggest audience for its series of books on filmmaking was for entry-level personnel, film students, and industry people trying to polish their skills. So, with this in mind, I went to a book store and looked over the selection of books available on the Costume Department. What I found were books that explained period fashions and theatrical costume construction techniques; what I didn't find was a book that told you how to breakdown a script for wardrobe department requirements for a film or TV show, and how to use that information to construct a wardrobe budget that you could present to any producer. Nor did I find one that explained the various concept styles of theatrical costume design, or explained running a department as a Designer, in other words, a book that gave you "real world" insights and information about a real job that you might be starting. Well, that's the book I've tried to write.

First thoughts: My experience is that, while many people feel they are capable, and have a desire to be theatrical Costume Designers, they don't realize that in order to be successful, apart from personal ability, they have to have a successful department behind them, one that is able to:

1) Handle the financial responsibilities of the department.
2) Be able to provide and maintain the costumes required.
3) Be able to work the clothes in front of camera.
4) Know how to wrap the department with no loose ends.

I've tried to address all that, chapter by chapter. Also, I've tried to separate the job requirements in their own chapters, chronologically... that is, from the time you decide to become a Costume Designer, to getting the job, to the order of how a show works, from the time you get a script; this means that some information is repeated from various angles at different times in the process, but this way, anyone can look up a specific area, or just read the book straight through.

Costume design and department supervision aren't as daunting or overwhelming as they might be, if you keep a few things in mind:

- People no smarter than you do it successfully.
- What you don't know, you can learn.
- It's all based on organization.

ACKNOWLEDGMENTS AND THANKS

In preparing new material for this edition I sought some outside advice. The role of Technical Advisor has grown over the years and I asked the most famous TA of all, Captain Dale Dye, to talk about the roll of Costume Designer; from his point of view; he did. His contribution is inserted at the end of the chapter on Costume Design. Captain Dye's credits include: *Platoon*, *Last of the Mohicans*, *Band of Brothers*, *Saving Private Ryan*, *Pacific*, *Alexander the Great*, and many others.

I also added a new chapter on television and asked a long-time friend, Loree Parral, to throw in some advice. She did. Loree is a 30-year veteran who's been nominated for several Emmys for costumes and won two, for such shows as: *L.A. Law*, *Picket Fences*, *Ally McBeal*, *The Practice,* and *Boston Legal*.

Working in Australia, I met a wonderful English Designer/Supervisor named Jo Korer. I asked her if she could think of anything to contribute and she wrote some advice on foreign location shooting which appears in chapter 18, on Shooting.

I also want to thank Edward Marks, president of Western Costume, and Diana Foster, president of American Costume, for adding their thoughts. Further, I'd like to thank Maria Lorenzana, costume designer/instructor, Mary Routh, costume designer/instructor, and Rachael Stanley, assistant executive director, Local #892. I am grateful to all of them.

PERSONAL INTRODUCTION

I got into the film industry the old fashioned way: nepotism. My mother, Lucy, was a world class cutter-fitter. She made dresses for ice shows, burlesque houses, stage reviews, personal sales and the movies, including gowns worn in *Gone with the Wind*. For years, she worked with Edith Head, realizing in cloth, what Edith created on paper. Of course, after growing up surrounded by seamstresses (some years the workroom at Paramount was my day care center), I developed an undying love for their skill and an inside appreciation of the problems of the workroom and costume manufacture.

I believe that all Designers should be able to draw as a way of communicating ideas to the people they have to work with. A few quick sketches in front of a director or production designer are truly worth a thousand words — talking over a quick sketch or "cartoon" with the person who has to make the costume is a real necessity. Later I'll get into simple ways to learn to make sketches for presentations.

My final great career shaper was a stint in the Marine Corps. I joined after high school in the early '60s and soon learned the meaning of the Marine motto, "Gung-Ho," Chinese for "work together." The Corps taught me several applicable lessons, among them:

- No organization works without a clear chain of command.
- Leadership is most effective when done from the front.
- Planning is central to the success of any mission.
- Good moral is invaluable for sustaining team effort in the face of adversity.
- A unit's (department's) ability and flexibility in meeting the challenges of changing situations is reliant on the efficient organization of its supplies.
- In all situations, determination, clear thinking, and quick decision making based on good information will be the deciding factors.

x

All these principles become very helpful when applied to filmmaking.

I got out of the Marine Corps in 1965 and started to work at Fox. It was the last days of the "studio system," when studios made their own films and ran huge lot departments to facilitate them.

The wardrobe department occupied several buildings and storage spaces. My job as "stock clerk" was: Learn where and what everything was (miles of clothes). Shine shoes and boots. Block and clean hats. Help costumers pull garments for their shows. Measure, size, and put away all returning clothing (truck loads of them).

Doing "returns" means going through the costume inventory of a show, item-by-item, looking for damages, while checking the items against the original "billing sheets" for losses, then breaking-down (separating) the stock and sending out the cleaning. Upon the cleaners' return, sizing (that is measuring) the clothes, tagging them and returning them to their place of storage, usually by period and type of garment. Spending weeks or months doing this is very instructive. You can see how different Costumers and Designers use the same clothes in various combinations for different effects. How selection and over-dyeing had developed various color schemes. How cleverly planned manufacture, dovetailed into existing stock, gives a "new" look. You can see costs related to repairable damages that could have been avoided and most of all, you learn to appreciate an organized return.

As I was starting out, I had the good fortune to apprentice under an older costume department head named Dick James. He mentored me with humorous sternness. His advice was, "Rich, this is a wonderful business... you can do anything you want, travel, make good money, meet wonderful people... only two things you can't do: Never be late, never make a mistake." While funny, this proved to be true.

As the costumers developed some confidence in me they would request that I assist them in "pulling" their shows. At Fox in the '60s, the senior costumers had been there since the '30s and had done shows such as *Viva Zapata* and *The Grapes of Wrath*, many times without Designers. In those early days, Designers usually came onto shows only when manufacture was expected, doing the dresses for the leading ladies or changes for the male cast, (except in the case of some musicals, where almost everything was designed). Rarely did Designers stick around for the whole show, as is the norm now.

"Pulling a show" consisted of helping to assemble the costumes that would be used on a project under the direction of the Costume Supervisor, who had been assigned the show by the studio department head. These old guys were tough task-masters but knew more about wardrobe, periods, and the basic nuts and bolts of running a show than anybody else; it was an eye-opening training ground into the realities of production. They were masters at the art of film production and anticipating the problems that would be a normal part of any film. Their forte was the creation of strong "character" wardrobe with its attendant jobs of aging and distressing. They were dedicated researchers who assessed every piece of wardrobe on its historical, as well as artistic, merits. Of course, some were better at it than others, but one only has to watch the clothes in those films made from the '20s to the '50s (and many later) to see how good they were. Sadly, they go largely unrecognized, because in those days nobody from wardrobe got screen credit except Designers and studio department heads.

My department progress followed the course of many. I was, next, fed out on lot shows as Set Costumer (TV's *Batman*, for one). I then worked several shows as "Key Set." Eventually the department decided that I was ready for a show of my own as Supervisor. Finally, a director named John Milius offered me a position as Costume Designer on a film he was to shoot in Spain. *The Wind and the Lion* was a real adventure for me and is still one of my favorite movies to watch.

That was a long time ago. Since then I have worked many films, television movies-of-the-week (MOWs), pilots, and series as both Costumer and Costume Designer. In practical terms, that means that I've had thousands of opportunities to make decisions about what people would wear on film and have been able to see the effects of those choices on the screen.

I've had the opportunity to supervise wardrobe departments in several foreign countries and several states on locations. I've owned my own business and have overseen the manufacture of hundreds of garments. I've also worked for several large costume houses as in-house shopper, buyer, designer, stock department head, and/or rentals, and customer service.

I've also made mistakes at every level of job I've ever had but, like the experience of most people, those mistakes taught me valuable lessons about both myself and my job.

Today, the business is different than when I started, so the training ground isn't always there anymore, for up-and-coming people to learn the ropes from an older generation of seasoned professionals. A lot of the people I see today struggle through shows because of this lack of opportunity for mentorship. I don't know if I can help anyone do a better job, or if I can really give anyone the benefit of my experience, but I'm happy to try... after all, we're all in the same department.

Costume for Sean Connery
The Wind and the Lion

chapter 1

THE ROLE OF THE COSTUME DESIGNER IN FILM AND TELEVISION

The short answer is to make sure the right clothes get on the right people at the right time.

The modern Costume Designers Guild came into existence in the 1950s (my membership number was #74). Before that, there were a few studio staff Costume Designers; others would be called out from Broadway on a show-by-show basis, usually to do stars' costumes or large-scale musicals, while the bulk of the shows' costumes were delivered by the Wardrobe Department Supervisors.

I think the best way to explain the jobs, by industry standards, is to let the Costume Designer Guild (Local #892, Hollywood) speak for itself. The following definition is from the Costume Designer Handbook (and printed here with the kind permission of Costume Designers Local #892). Local #892 is an "International" union and represents people the world over. To find out more information or contact them, go to: *www. costumedesignersguild.com.*

THE COSTUME DESIGNER:
Determines the look of a production by designing the costumes. Although each job has slightly different requirements, here is a list of potential duties:

- Helps Production select a Costume Supervisor, Assistant Designer and/or Illustrator.
- Read and breakdown the script.

- Script analysis and character delineation & progression. Define special requirements of script as it pertains to costumes. Preliminary budget to be drafted with Costume Supervisor.
- Research.
  Research materials appropriate to the project.
- Creative Development.
  Develop a design concept.
  Meet with actor, producer, and director.
  Determine which garments should be selected from existing garments.
  Determine which garments should be constructed.
  Sketching (Full renderings, line drawings, thumbnail sketches, working drawings).
  Collaborate with production team.
- Attend preproduction meetings.
- Interface with producers, directors, and actors.
- Realize the design.
  Ability to explain to Workroom how costume is to be constructed.
  Knowledge of appropriate fabrics.
  Follow the creation of the costume from inception to completion.
  Shop as needed for clothing, accessories, and fabrics.
  Rent costumes as needed.
  Communicate your design ideas to your crew.
- Oversee the fittings.
  Communicate design to cutter/fitter and staff.
  Communicate your design concept to the actor.
- One member of the Finished Costume Group (L.A. 705) is to be present at a fitting. Please note that the Costume Supervisor is not required to be at the fitting.
- One member of the Custom-made Group (tailor staff) must be present at a fitting where pinning is done.
- Approve fitting photos.

DURING FILM PRODUCTION:

- Establish the look of the character.
- Change the look of the character, if necessary.
- Maintain the integrity of the look of the show.
- Create looks for day and featured players.
- Make decisions for the next day's filming.
- Keep abreast of script changes.
- Set the look of extras.

ASSISTANT COSTUME DESIGNER:

An Assistant Costume Designer can do everything that a Costume Designer can do, except design independently of the Costume Designer.

Every working situation is different and every relationship between Costume Designer, Assistant Costume Designer and Costume Supervisor is uniquely defined by their specific strengths, therefore, this list of possible duties may vary from show to show. Much also depends upon the staffing of the rest of the department and some of these duties may be shared with the Costume Supervisor. Please consider this list as a guideline while evaluating the ways that an Assistant Costume Designer may contribute to a project.

- Assisting with script analysis and character delineation and progression.
- Developing a list of costumes with Designer.
  Defining the special requirements of the script as it pertains to the costumes.
- Research.
  Period history, history of costume construction.
  Uniforms (i.e. police, jail, military, etc.).
  Contemporary styles (fashion).
  Regional variances.
  Social mores, etiquette.
  New materials.

3

- Creative Development.
  Serving as a second set of eyes and ears at creative meetings.
  Sketching, if needed.
  Color analysis.
  Coordination with prop master to establish cross-over list.
  Serving as liaison with the Special Effects Department.
  Serving as liaison with the Hair and Make-up Department.
  Serving as liaison with the stunt coordinator, making sure the costumes accommodate the stunt work.
- Footwork. (Calling upon interpersonal relationships, knowledge of sources and suppliers)
  Swatching fabrics.
  Knowledge of fabrics and textiles.
  Knowledge of textile history and its application to period costumes.
  Knowledge of construction as it bears on the selection of fabrics.
  Shopping with a creative eye to protect the integrity of the Designer's vision.
  Assuming some telephone responsibilities to alleviate the Designer's workload.
  Knowledge of rental houses and their stock.
- Made-to-order (Often referred to as "M.O.").
  Following the creation of the costume from inception to completion.
  Liaison between the Designer and the Workroom.
  Ability to read and interpret sketches.
  Making sure the cutters and crafts persons have everything they need, every day.
  Ability and authority to make impromptu decisions when the Designer is unavailable.
- Fittings.
  Assisting the Designer to set up fitting rooms and organize costumes.
  Taking notes and photos during fittings.
  Assisting in any way during fittings (Knowing when to speak and when to be silent).
  Helping to make the actor feel comfortable.

ADDITIONAL DUTIES ONCE FILMING BEGINS:
- Fittings.
- Extras — approving fittings in the absence of the Designer to maintain consistency of design.
- Day and featured players — sometimes create looks for these actors when the Designer is not present.
- Specialty Scenes — putting together special combinations of clothes under the Designer's supervision.
- Keeping the home fires burning while the rest of the staff is on location.
- Prepping ahead.
- Putting costumes to work in Los Angeles shops.
- Shipping costumes and supplies to location.
- Keeping abreast of script changes.
- Keeping in touch with casting.
- Filling in for the Designer on set when creative questions arise and the Designer is not available.

The additional job classifications presided over by the Designers Guild are:

ILLUSTRATOR:
- Translate verbal concept of character into an illustration.
  Types of illustrations:
  1. Presentation illustration.
  2. Technical illustration for Workroom to build from.

STYLIST / COMMERCIAL COSTUME DESIGNER (Obsolete, reference only):
Commercial Costume Designer is the term used in the Producer's Contract for the Costume Designers Guild; however, the term most commonly used within the industry is Stylist.
- A Stylist/Designer typically works on either commercials or music videos.
- A Stylist/Commercial Costume Designer is allowed to build original costumes as well as shop, rent, fit, and alter existing costumes.

COMMERCIALS:

- The Commercial Stylist/Designer is expected to create and provide all costumes that may be required for the production of a television commercial.
- The director's production company hires the Stylist/Designer.
- The Stylist/Designer works with the director, producer, advertising agency, client, and actors to create a look appropriate to selling an idea or product.

The elements/procedures that may be implemented during the course of production are as follows:

- Reviews the storyboards and/or script for the commercial.
- Makes a visual, or verbal, presentation of design ideas based on information provided.
- Reviews the production schedule: amount of prep time, booking of cast, number of shoot days, number of wrap days, and budget.
- Hires crew for Costume Department.
- Arranges for all shopping, pulling from rental houses, and construction of garments to be ready for scheduled fittings.
- Arranges for all overseas fittings with actors.
- Presents the recommended costume choices to the director, the advertising agency creative team, and the client for approval.

DURING THE FILMING:

- The Stylist/Designer is responsible for all costume needs during the shoot: this may entail last-minute changes, dressing of extras, upkeep of costumes.

WRAP:

After completion of shooting, the Stylist/Designer is expected to arrange for:

- Return of costumes to appropriate vendors.
- Inventory purchases (which are usually the property of the advertising agency or the company upon completion of the job).
- Completing all paperwork related to the Costume Department.

6

The key element necessary for a successful experience as a Designer in commercial advertising may be a "Clarity of Design Vision" coupled with a logical and amenable flexibility in both work style and design ideas.

The process of commercial production is very much a collaborative venture between the Stylist/Commercial Costume Designer, the director, and the advertising agency creative team.

MUSIC VIDEOS:

- The music video Stylist/Designer is expected to create and provide all costumes that may be required for the production of the music video.
- Music videos are more of a crossover between a film and selling a product.
- The artist is your product, and will be much more involved in the creative process.
- Most often, in music videos, there is a story line or visual concept to follow.
- Each video may have its own set of costume challenges.

DURING MUSIC VIDEO PRODUCTION:

- The creative team may also include the artist featured in the video.
- The production scheduling for a music video may be similar to commercial scheduling, but the creative involvement of the Stylist/Designer may be similar to a film.

WRAP:

After completion of shooting, the Stylist/Designer is expected to arrange for:

- Return of costumes to appropriate vendors.
- Inventory purchases (which are usually the property of the artist or the production company upon completion of the job).
- Completing all paperwork related to the department.

7

The following job descriptions are from Motion Picture Costumers, Local #705, which is divided into different divisions:

- Finished Costumers: Key Costumer (known as Costume Supervisor), Journeyman, Entry Level, Commercials.
- Custom Made: 5 Classes in both Men's and Women's Groups.
- Costume House Employees.
- Live Television Costumers.

In Local #705 there is a specific division of job classifications:

- Finished Costumer is allowed to handle completed garments for any production.
- A finished Costumer cannot fit, alter, or manufacture garments.
- Custom Made Costumers fit, alter, and/or manufacture garments.
- Costume House Employees work in a Costume House.
- Live Television Costumers only work in live television.

COSTUME SUPERVISOR:

A Costume Supervisor can do everything that a Costume Designer and an Assistant Costume Designer can do, except design.

- The Costume Supervisor should start a job when there are costumes to be handled, purchased, or rented.

A Costume Supervisor is a job title for a person who is classified in #705 as a Key Costumer. It's a bit confusing because there is not a #705 union classification for Costume Supervisor, but there is a Costume Supervisor classification in the Producer's Contract with #705. The Costume Supervisor (Key Costumer) is a person who has completed work as a Journeyman Costumer for 400 days within a four-year period, has paid the reclassification fee, and has been placed on the producer's roster as a Key Costumer.

THE COSTUME SUPERVISOR MANAGES THE COSTUME DEPARTMENT:

- The Costume Supervisor is familiar with each aspect of a project.
- The Costume Supervisor is responsible for the smooth operation of the Costume Department.

- Department meetings will help to determine each Costumer's specific tasks.
- The Costume Supervisor maintains communication with all other departments.
- The Costume Supervisor monitors the budget at all times, communicating information as needed.
- The Costume Supervisor runs the crew.

THE SUPERVISOR IN PREPRODUCTION:

- Is responsible for script breakdown.
- Works with Designer in budgeting.
- Assists in procuring research.
- Sets up the department.
- Sets up offices, Workroom, and trailer.
- Opens accounts for needed services and vendors.
- Coordinates fitting schedules with the Designer, the actor, the Workroom, and the Production Office.
- Hires the crew with the Designer's input.

THE SUPERVISOR DURING PRODUCTION:

- Keeps in close contact with the shooting company, regarding schedules.
- Is aware of the needs of the production so that changes can be accommodated and delays eliminated.
- Maintains constant monitoring of expenses and budget tracking.
- Informs producers when unanticipated changes will increase costume budget.
- Communicates all information to and from all members of the Costume Department.
- Continues an open relationship with actors and production personnel.

THE COSTUME SUPERVISOR IN POSTPRODUCTION:

- Returns all wardrobe to the appropriate space, in good condition, well labeled, and organized.
- Insures all accounting is complete.
- Turns in all set books to production.
- Completes inventory as needed.
- Verifies asset sheet.
- Thanks everyone, including vendors, for doing a great job.

If a Costume Supervisor is hired on a production that does not have a Costume Designer, the Costume Supervisor can do everything a Costume Designer would do, except design.

- A Supervisor can copy garments that exist but there are rules regarding this.
- Please refer to the Agreement between Motion Picture Costumers #705 and Costume Designers Guild #892, regarding copying (re-manufacturing) jurisdiction or call the locals for details. The basic gist of the contract provides that direct copying to create multiple costumes is appropriate to both #705 and #892 members — but this is a simplification — if in doubt, check with either union.

THE SET COSTUMER:

The Set Costumer is the front line of communication between the set and the Costume Department.

THE SET COSTUMER IN PREPRODUCTION:

- Becomes completely familiar with the script, the breakdown, and the costumes.
- Assists in organizing the workspace so that it is beneficial to everyone.
- Anticipates needs that may occur during shooting in addition to on-camera costumes.
- Prepares an on-set work kit in an effort to avoid any costume-related production delays.

10

DURING PRODUCTION THE SET COSTUMER:
- Sets the costumes for the day's work.
- Maintains all wardrobe and accessories.
- Must know the status of the day's work and be constantly vigilant to all aspects of the production.
- Maintains the set book by taking accurate photos and wardrobe continuity notes.
- **Reports any changes or surprises** immediately to the Costume Supervisor and/or Costume Designer.
- Takes good care of actors.

A careful reading of the above union-sanctioned job definitions gives a straight-forward laundry list of job requirements and responsibilities. Whether you work in Hollywood on a union production or in another state or country not covered by this union contract — the job will remain the same and fall into three general phases: 1). Getting the clothes; 2). Working the clothes to camera; 3). Returning the clothes at the wrap.

1880 scout
book illustration, *Indian Scouts*, John Langelier

chapter 2

GETTING IN
THE BUSINESS

The nature of Costume Design is entrepreneurial, as well as artistic. Staff jobs at major studios are rare. The most common way to work is show to show. There are people who work television for a season at a time and sometimes several seasons in a row — but eventually the show runs out. Some find employment with a certain producer — but often that producer moves to another job. So the first step toward getting into the business is to understand the nature of it, and prepare yourself for it.

As a Costume Designer you are selling a service and your ability to perform that service to the satisfaction of your client — the production company. You need to perform well enough that it results in referrals, as you build good client relationships with producers, directors, line producers, unit managers, and actors. Remember, you build your career by helping them build theirs.

Your ability to get a first job may come as a "lucky break" but your ability to take that job to a successful conclusion and build it into a career will be up to you, your dedication, skill, knowledge, and understanding of what to expect.

It often has been said that every job is a sales job. That is no less true with becoming a Costume Designer. In this case, the thing you are selling is you and the skill set you can bring to the table.

The specific job category and career path you choose will help determine how you prepare yourself. Think of it as this – "Target Marketing"...

1) If your ambition is to be a Costume Designer for film and you live in the Los Angeles or New York area (or any city in the world with a motion picture industry), you might decide to start by applying for interviews with recognized Costume Designers for work as Assistant, or you might try and advertise directly to production companies. Remember: most mainstream work is union and requires job experience, so you might have to confine your job searches to non-union and smaller independent production companies until you gain the experience and screen credits to join the Designers Guild. (Check for Costume Designers Guild policy.)

2) If you live in other areas of the country where film work is limited you may want to search out commercial/music video houses or the art departments of advertising firms.

Working for any company usually means being an employee versus an Independent Contractor. "Employee" can be a good thing as the employer pays into your Social Security and may offer other benefits including medical plans; plus, your work expenses are paid for by the company.

Being "Freelance" can be done in two ways:

1) Independent Employee — An Independent Employee is basically an "Employee for Hire." That means you will look for jobs like: films, commercials, or music videos that are temporary in nature and will work from show to show as a Costume Designer/Stylist. You might develop a portable department and charge the company a "Box Rental" for the use of the supplies that you bring to the job. In this case, you will search out vendors and perhaps open accounts with them. You will find other temporary crafts people, tailors, wardrobe labor, whom you can call to help you, as needed.

2) Independent Contractor — This job category is really a self-owned business. Working under this kind of contract means that the hiring company has no financial obligation to you for any employer share of tax payments, Social Security, or pension. The Internal Revenue Service has ruled that producers cannot hire labor to work on films as independent contractors. You can go on line and read the legalities. I would advise that you talk with an accountant before setting yourself up as an independent contractor. Remember, if you choose to work that way, whatever you're paid will be "gross" earnings and you will be subject to a +/- 15% to 30% loss of real income, paying your own employer share of benefits and taxes.

Most people work as employees, in which case you have a "fiduciary" duty to act in the best interest of your client/employer. That means that you are the agent and/or representative and can't "bump" any bills, take any "kick-backs" or "sales commissions" or engage in any "wholesale-retailing." Any favorable deals or pricing you get have to be passed on to the company you work for.

FINDING JOBS:

There are several places that sell listings for producers, production companies, commercial houses, costume houses, directors, agents, and worthwhile associations. These books can be found in major city bookstores and on line — as can the advertisements for the companies themselves. Many of these sources also publish upcoming production schedules. There are both film industry newspapers like *Variety, Hollywood Reporter,* and *Dramalog* and also trade magazines like *Filmmaker* and *Indie Slate*, where job information can be found. Also: *btlnews.com* and *findfilmwork.com*

CREATING A BUSINESS PERSONA:

(Persona — the personality you project in social situations.) By this I don't mean becoming a "phony," I mean crafting yourself into a professional person who can compete successfully in a highly competitive job market.

You have to prepare yourself with enough knowledge about what will be required to feel confident in a job interview (keep reading this book), and personal marketing material.

This is a position that demands attention to detail, promptness, artistic ability, and fiduciary responsibility and you have to *look* the part — it's all part of projecting yourself as the person for the job and gaining the confidence of a prospective employer. As they say, "you only get one chance to make a first impression" and this business is all about *appearance* and *presentation*.

PERSONAL MARKETING MATERIAL:

Résumés

Only show them what you want them to see. There are plenty of books written on various formats for résumés. I have received many and can tell you that there are two mistakes I see most often:

1) Résumés that are filled with lots of information not applicable to the job, or are short on experience, but long on mission statement.

2) The other kind is too "artsy," too cute. Of the two, I gravitate towards the "artsy" ones, but I really prefer something that doesn't try too hard to convince me, and just tells me about the person and relevant experience/education. I always respond to a well-done costume sketch that is somehow included.

Again, your résumé is your first impression *personal presentation*. What does it say about you? Your choices about yourself, your level of seriousness and artistic sensibilities? A résumé is generally considered a list of your education, job aspirations, and experience.

PORTFOLIO:

In the beginning your portfolio will contain the sample work you develop during your education process. As you progress, your portfolio will grow with new sketches and/or photographs of costumes you have had made and shows you have worked on — this might evolve into a DVD reel.

The intention of a portfolio is to show prospective clients and employers your skill level and the kind of design work they can expect from you, if you are hired. You can see how important a good portfolio is and why you should take full advantage of school time and projects to develop one. Portfolios contain examples of your conceptual design projects — traditionally sketches that are swatched — and also manufactured projects that exemplify your abilities. This means that you MUST work on your drawing as a means of communicating your ideas. (More on that later.)

BROCHURES:

Brochures are more artistically articulated than résumés and are designed to be disseminated as advertising and promotional material. Brochures can be left with the interviewing people or mailed out to prospective employers. Brochures usually include a mix of résumé and portfolio work in an artistic presentation.

Burning CDs is the newer way to send out a brochure with style. They take effort and money to produce but they can make a strong impression about your dedication and business savvy.

BUSINESS CARDS:

Your business cards should do the same thing. Attractively present yourself via color, paper choice, job description, font style, and so on.

WEBSITES:

Websites are getting easier to put together. You can go online and see what other people are doing. It may not be too important in the beginning, but as you network in the business and develop a reputation, your website will become more and more necessary, acting as an online résumé/portfolio that you can direct clients to.

POST CARDS:

There are companies that create post cards for mass mailings. You can have your art work printed on a card and sent out to whatever list you want. Mailing lists can be purchased or culled from unions and trade resource material.

PRINT ADS:

Depending on your area and target field, you might consider running print advertisements in trade magazines, newspapers, telephone books — wherever your clients might find you.

COLD CALLING:

This simply means calling potential clients/employers, introducing yourself, and requesting job information. If you're going to do this, work out a script first. It may sound corny but have your relevant information in front of you — there's nothing worse than getting in a good job contact call and stumbling around, searching for something to say — or hanging up and remembering something important that you wanted to say, but forgot. Write it all down.

Whichever way you choose to advertise yourself, be persistent and patient. Some people like to put their photographs on their marketing materials. Why? So that when you make follow-up calls, the people you're talking to can put a face and a name with the voice. You're creating relationships.

17

General Jackson's Wife
Gods and Generals

chapter 3

THE JOB INTERVIEW

Okay! You've studied, you feel confident, you have designed and constructed a résumé/brochure, sent your marketing material out, made follow-up calls and you've found a company that wants to interview you — Now what?

While every job situation and meeting is different, imagine yourself as a producer — you have a project to shoot and you're looking for someone to manage the costumes. You don't want any mistakes. You don't want it to cost too much. You want a good job. You are busy but will take a few minutes to interview a few people — the first one is here now. Now imagine that *you* come through the door. How do you look? How do you act? What makes you want to hire the person you see?

Attitude is everything. The best advice I ever had on interviews came from a real estate trainer — he said that when going for a listing he always opened with this: "Hi, I'm here today to look into this job and I certainly appreciate your taking the time to see me. I just want to tell you that when this interview is over I know that one of three things will happen: You'll hire me and I'll work hard to make it a win-win deal; You'll get somebody else and we'll keep in touch for the future; or, I'll decide that this job isn't for me because I can't meet your expectations." (Which usually means the pay isn't enough or there's not enough money in their budget to do the job they want.) Now, of course, you don't have to say this, but you can think it.

The purpose of the interview is to get the job — but the purpose of the job is to be in a realistic work situation. Sometimes the work situations are not realistic. You have to be able to stand off a little, emotionally, and decide if the job you're interviewing for is really the job you want, with the conditions that you are willing to accept — that translates into the hours of work demanded (usually between 12 and 18 hours a day), the amount of help allowed and the pay received. Sometimes it doesn't matter because you just want the opportunity. That's okay, just decide it ahead of time.

A professional attitude is usually based on two things: First is confidence — the self knowledge that you have what the other person needs, by way of your job skill, and second, confidence in your ability to present yourself as the person they will *want* to work with.

Remember, at first they don't know you, so everything's based on their perceptions of you — if your professional image as Designer (presentation) doesn't meet the client's perception of the image of a Designer, then they are less likely to hire you.

Professional sales people — people whose livelihoods depend on making sales — have developed many strategies for successful interviews and meetings that can be boiled down to a few simple rules:

1) Know what your customers want and give it to them.

2) Know what you're selling and be enthusiastic about it.

3) Talk benefits, not cost.

4) Be honest, sincere, ethical, and positive — no matter what.

One common way to prepare for a meeting is to practice what you're going to say. Write a list of reasons why you will be a good hire — things about your business ethic, enjoyment of the job, and qualifications and say them to yourself in the mirror until you can do it with confidence. Practicing with another person asking you impromptu questions is another way to sharpen your interview skills; after all, if you go to a hundred interviews you will be asked many of the same questions, time after time. Try to have the answers ready.

An additional strategy is to research the firm and/or person you will interview with. Look them up online, familiarizing yourself with their industry history, the type of work they do and have done. Know whom you're talking to.

The last sales tip is to always try and be the last one seen. After your interview simply ask, "Before you make up your mind I'd like a chance for a final interview." The reason is simple, you are fresh on their minds and have an opportunity to overcome final objections when they're closest to hiring.

★*Final Note:* After you've done a few shows you may be tempted to relate a prior bad experience on a job interview. Don't! If you speak ill about a prior experience the person you're talking to will understand that you may speak badly about him or her in the future to someone else — a sure job loser.

Cowgirl concept,
Shaunessy

chapter **4**

THE DEAL

Regarding the Deal: if your situation is a union one then payment is proscribed by established contract (until you reach the level of industry-recognized professional, when your services can command more than contract wages).

As you start work you will be asked to sign a "Deal Memo." That Deal Memo becomes the basic contract between you and the company and will spell out your wages and any and all other contract considerations between you and the hiring company.

You usually will have to negotiate your deal with the unit manager or line producer. The word "negotiate" scares some people but a negotiation is simply the process of talking about an exchange of value until all parties are in acceptance.

I'm not a lawyer or an agent. I used to have an agent; he always got me more than I would have gotten for myself, and, his intervention in the deal-making process sheltered me from entering into a potentially adversarial relationship with the production company over pay for services — always a bad way to start. Some of the things he always addressed were:

> **Screen Credits:** "Costume Designer" — On a film, he always asked for an "Up Front, Single Card" credit (Television productions under union contract have rules that may prohibit this). Additionally, he would ask for my credits to appear on all print and advertising material (DVD boxes and posters).

Car Use: In-town car allowance and on-location car rental.

Travel: Lodging and Per Diem (on location), "Favored Nations" with the production designer (art director in advertising). The production designer is usually hired by the time they hire you and that deal has already been agreed upon, so tying your deal to his or hers as a fellow designer is a fair and acceptable practice.

Box Rental: (paid weekly.) What are you going to bring, if anything? Sewing machines, set kit and tools, computer and printer, art supplies, research? Whatever it is, the company will want an evaluated inventory for insurance purposes.

Wages: The position of Costume Designer is sometimes considered, "Management" and "On Call," which means that you're paid a "flat" amount per week, not on an hourly basis. How many hours do you expect to work on the job? A regular shooting day can be 12 hours, plus the time before and after to dress and wrap the talent. A five-day schedule could be 60 hours or more (the most hours I ever worked in a week was 120 in six days). I can't recommend a wage scale. There are rate books that give union contract wages. They are updated by contract and would be obsolete soon after this book is published. Also, as a non-union person, the wage is based on the size and budget of the project and the area of the country the work takes place in. Starting out, you just have to ask yourself if the pay offer is worth the job and if you're going to derive the benefit you need. Later, in the budget section, we'll go over how to figure out if the budget will support you and what you feel you need to do the show.

Day Provision: If the shooting week is scheduled for five days and your rate is based on that, what happens if you have to work six or seven days? The sixth day can be pro-rated (the same daily rate as the first five) with the seventh day to be a "double-time day" (or time-and-a-half). On union shows there are demanded hours between calls — that means that you *have* to have at least six hours between quitting and reporting back (it varies, union by union).

Work Developed: Companies usually specify in their contracts that they own everything you do during the course of working on their projects, which includes your sketches and any costumes you supervise the construction of. If you include a line that you wish to be able to use any and all of your work contributions for your personal, *non-commercial*, marketing use, they should agree and you will be free to use copies of your sketches and photographs of your work in your promotional material. (Studios might exclude star actor specialty costumes.) This becomes more and more valuable to you as you develop a body of work for your website, résumés, and brochures.

DISNEY

26

Dance Couple concept
Disneyland

chapter 5

PROGRAMMING AND FIRST PRESENTATIONS

Every production happens differently and there is no set sequence of events in preproduction. This stage is helpful to everyone but sometimes, owing to time and/or availability, it may be more or less formal.

PROGRAMMING:

Once interviewed and hired, you may be given a script to read with the thought that when you've read it, you will have a "concept meeting" with the director. The purpose of this meeting is to get yourself on track with the creative thinking of production. (There is another section on reading the script in more detail, so some of this information will be reiterated later.)

Your first reading of the script is for general feeling. What's the period, the mood (level of drama) and who are the main characters?

You may be asked to submit your thoughts on how you "see" the show and how you would proceed — but, this meeting shouldn't concern budget. This meeting should be to gather the information that a later budget will be based on.

The first meeting should give you an opportunity to ask questions of the director and, with hope, the production designer. What you're trying to find out is how do other people with a creative responsibility "visualize" the project. Do they have any art references that you can see? Any films that you should view? Do they have any *inspiration* for this project that you can take a cue from?... (Books, artists, old films).

Here is where you want to ask questions and take notes. How will the overall lighting be — light or dark? Is there any thought on color palette?

What's *important* to the director, visually? What do they want to *say*? Who's the intended audience?

Armed with this information, you construct your *first concept presentation*.

★I know that I've lost at least a couple of jobs because I was too excited about presenting my ideas and didn't exercise my better judgment during this phase, which should be about discovery — that means listening to *their* ideas.

How you plan to deliver this presentation will determine how you construct it.

The most popular methods are:

1. Live, in the office at a meeting.
2. Via the Internet by PowerPoint presentation.
3. By submitted CD.

Meetings used to always happen in person. I like this system better because it's personal and gives everyone a chance to comment and ask questions about the material presented. However, today, some production companies ask to have first presentations delivered electronically to save time and be more convenient for their viewing schedules.

There is a later section that deals with script breakdown and character development, so we'll assume that you have made the basic decisions on what your ideas are, concerning these elements; the question at this stage is how to best present your ideas about your concept.

The **concept presentation** is a first-pass **art/design presentation** backed up by relevant research. This presentation isn't intended to get too specific, but to gain acceptance for a design direction. While there are no perfect rules, some of the things you will have to address are:

1. The main characters.
2. The general "feel" for the background.
3. The "overall" color sense.
4. Relevant research.

This presentation might include: Photocopied pages from art and/ or costume books, original sketches, swatches, color chips, photographs of costumes, and anything else that you feel conveys your ideas.

If your presentation is "live" you might consider creating "Design Boards" on foam core; it's stronger than poster board and will stand up better by itself. Using black board offers a good contrast to your presented work. Foam core board comes in various sizes and the tri-fold boards are a good size and manageable. Remember, you'll have to carry these in and out of offices, so the more portable, the better. You might investigate a small two-wheeled cart for transport.

The presentation can be organized in any manner you think most suits the concept material you have developed, but you might consider one board for research, one for main characters (or one for each leading character) and one for crowd types, by set.

Implicit in each concept is suggested color and texture — arrived at by a combination of original art work, photocopied research and swatches. How you put these elements together will allow you to express not only your concepts but also your overall design and presentation skills, as well as your understanding of the project.

★These design boards are good but they can grow to burdensome amounts. If you start to put everything from every meeting on these boards you will soon have stacks of boards to keep track of and carry around. I would suggest that once approved, you digitally photograph them and mount the photos in protective plastic sheets in a three ring binder(s). The information can then be copied. Duplicates can be given to costumers pulling costumes or used in the fitting room for research while you have the originals to take to meetings.

Other ways to submit your design presentation are: By PowerPoint, viewed on a laptop computer in the production office. This is basically the same as presenting by board. You might either scan in material or make up boards and photograph them, then scan the digital photos.

Submitted by email or CD, some production companies ask for a "First Impression" *before* you're hired. The only concern here is that you don't know who will look at it, what they think about it or what they will do with it later. This can be worrisome if you include original artwork which might represent valuable design ideas that someone could take advantage of, without hiring you.

In the end it's better to present in person and be able to explain, hear feedback, and take your material with you when you leave.

Concept

chapter **6**

SETTING UP
THE DEPARTMENT

You got the job and have started your "Preparation Period" — Preproduction. What are your first goals?

Get help! Some Designers prefer to start with an Assistant to help accumulate research, swatch, make calls, etc. Many (myself included) start by getting the most experienced Supervisor available. Like any social adventure, running a department on production is a study in relationships. The first relationship, and in my book, the most important, is the relationship between Designer and Supervisor.

Your situation is this: The production clock is ticking. You have from now until the first day of shooting to: research the costumes, make a "breakdown/budget package," come up with a concept for the cast, get all that approved, set up a physical department, assess and hire costumer help, accumulate costumes for cast and background by shopping, renting, and overseeing manufacture, have cast fittings and alterations, get them approved, complete costume house billing, arrange for payment, get everything packed and shipped to location, set up a location department, have final cast and background fittings, complete aging and distressing, and ready location transportation.

Some projects are small, some large, some mind-boggling and your prep time may be four months or two weeks — your costumes may all be available from a local thrift store or require massive manufacture — but your primary department mission will stay the same: get the right clothes in front of camera the day they work.

31

The Designer may be hired first and be considered the Department Head, but as the old saying goes: "it's not how smart you are that counts, it's how smart you hire." You're not expected to work alone and you shouldn't want to micro-manage department labor.

The union of Designer and Supervisor is thought of as: The Designer does the art and the Super does the business — or, the Designer does the "look" and the Super makes it happen.

The Designer wants to be free to devote his or her time to the cast, while the Supervisor sets up and runs the department.

The running of the department is the job of the Supervisor and an experienced one will know who, how, and what is needed to get the job done — that's why it's important to partner-up early, to plan the show together with the Supervisor and create a realistic budget based on both your assessments of what the show will require.

It's possible to do both jobs at once — lots of us have done it, but to do that you need a small show or must be *very* experienced in where to spend your time and where to get things.

Interview early, find someone you're comfortable with, hopefully someone with experience on a similar project. If you have to pull this job off by yourself, hire the most trusted, smart, and organized person you can find, have him or her read the Supervisor job description in Chapter One and work it out together.

Depending on the size of your show you may have several people in your department including costumers and sewers. If you accept the position of Department Head, you can demand that they do their best work, but you owe them strong and benevolent leadership, plus all the tools and information they need to do the job you expect of them, including a well-thought-out design plan. If any of them has to make an on-the-spot decision without you, you want it to be based on a shared understanding of your preferred design direction. Sometimes people don't work out and you have to let someone go – if that's the case, do it quickly and in private.

First to do: Start a work schedule with calendar-production dates and a "To-Do" list. Next: Create a department business plan.

ICLAND OF
DOCTOR MOREAU

BARBARA CARRERA

DINNER

33

Costume for Barbara Carrera
The Island of Dr. Moreau

3PC TEL LINEN SUIT
IBC CUTAWAY.

ISLAND OF
DACTOR MOREAU
BURT LANCASTER
CH# 1

Costume for Burt Lancaster
The Island of Dr. Moreau

chapter *7*

SCRIPT BREAKDOWN

READING THE SCRIPT FOR THE DEPARTMENT: ASSESSING REQUIREMENTS AND DEVELOPING BUDGET MATERIAL.

You read the script with two objectives in mind:

First, to assess the requirements for the department.

Both Designer and Supervisor are interested in the same things — how "big" is the project, what's the period, what's the level of drama? The difference is that the Designer sees and thinks in terms of color, detail, and specific costumes while the Supervisor is more interested in crowd size, amount of cast, length of schedule, difficulty of locations, and logistics.

Second, to arrive at a department budget.

That is, to try and predict a final department cost that can be discussed with the producers and accountants. Another way to think of your breakdown package is this: let's say that you're going into a business of your own. It's a start-up operation.

You want to borrow money from the bank to fund your idea. Your idea was to design, manufacture, and retail a line of clothing. You would need a diverse staff to perform many and varied functions, as well as office space and supplies, warehouse space and fixtures, manufacturing space and equipment, transportation, shipping and receiving. You anticipated hundreds of pieces of inventory to rotate through your facility daily, requiring a maintenance operation. Your expenditures would be ongoing, necessitating some sort of in-house accounting system. Your operation would exist over time, in various phases, each having its own related costs, and required expertise.

No matter how great a creative genius you were, before any banks would lend you any money to pursue your idea, they would demand that you submit, for their approval, a "Business Plan," and this business plan would have to show:

1. That *you* understood what you were getting yourself, and them, into, regarding time and money and…

2. That *you* were able to manage the work that you were suggesting.

Well, that's exactly what you're doing. Heading up a large department for a film company has all the same challenges and responsibilities as going into a small business — employees, inventory, payroll, physical work space… through time. So, the requirements that banks and businesses demand (financial responsibility combined with job insight), also are demanded by the producers and accountants who act as the "bank" on every film.

Okay, you're sitting at home, you had a great meeting with the producer and have been hired. You now have a fresh screenplay in your hand and are excited because it validates you as a costume professional. It represents another stepping stone in your career and you get to pay your rent for another three months. Well, what now?

Read it — that's right, no pressure, just read it.

Your first reading should be as innocent as the audience that will see it later. Scribble some notes: General impressions, things that stood out one way or another, what was the story about, what stood out about the main characters, any serious questions?

By the end of the script you should have a good gut feeling about what kind of film it is, how serious it is, the level of drama, what periods and locations it covers, how "big" a production it is. Before you can understand what's expected of you, you have to understand what kind of project it is. That overview will form the mental background for your subsequent discussions about the story with anyone.

*If you're going to have a concept meeting, you should develop a list of characters and their functions in the story, a list of major scenes and locations, and an idea about crowd types. This first reading will form the basis for your *concept presentation*.

When your design direction is approved you have to be ready to address a budget because that will be the subject of the next meeting with Production: What will these great ideas of yours cost?

You want to start to build a foundation on paper that will serve as reference material for everyone and everything that follows, until the end of production. That will include: breakdowns, research, and budget. In other words, your "**Costume Department Business Plan.**"

★I still work with a pencil and paper and that's how I'll explain things... but, if you're computer literate, all my information will transfer to a computer spreadsheet format. I like to see everything spread out on a table in front of me as I work on it. I tend to build it visually and physically at the same time. On a computer I can only see the page I'm working on until I print them all out... too long for me to wait. Having said that, there is a computer program that many in Hollywood (and in film schools) think is great. You can find information on it at: *www.prosanity.com*. I understand that there will have been an updated program available as of January, 2009, but the above named website will tell you what you need to know, including features and price.

I do two master breakdowns: the first is a "**Chronological**" breakdown, that is, I list the scenes in order by sequence (a sequence is a series of scenes that take place together; when the scenes change location or time, it's a new sequence). In each sequence I list the cast members who appear, as well as the types of background and a guess at the amounts of extras. I also list, briefly, the action and weather, if a factor. This breakdown will serve as a template for subsequent costume lists from which my budget will be derived.

While doing this breakdown I become very familiar with the story, sequence of events, cast, plot points, mood and action, as well as locations and the dramatic point the writer is trying to convey. In other words, what kind of film is it? How serious is it? How big is it? (All with an eye to how it should look.)

The next breakdown I make is called a "**Crossplot.**" It's made on graph paper and is very easy to do. A few lines across the top create categories that correspond to scene headings in the script: **Location; Day/Night; Interior/Exterior; Scene Number.** Down the vertical left-hand margin I number one through 20 (sometimes on larger shows I have to tape two pieces together and number down to 50, or more). Each number will correspond to an actor's "Cast Number" which the First Assistant will have on his or her strip board and which will appear on every daily call sheet under "cast requirements." (Having read the script I know who the main characters are and start with the most seen and work down.)

The bottom few lines I use for "background" or "atmosphere" and "stunts." For example, in a Western I would have lines for "townspeople — men," "townspeople – women," "cowboys", "Indians"… whatever main groups I will see with regularity in any amounts.

Now I read the script again, filling in the information boxes across the top of the page, and the cast down the vertical column. When I find that an actor or background group works in a particular scene, I put a "slash" in the box under that scene number. When there is a change of time, I separate that scene number from the next one with a vertical red pencil line. Soon the whole show is separated into chronological units.

You can see at a glance, in which scenes a character works, how many changes (day changes) they have, who is in the scene with them. You can see the "flow" of the show as well as the continuity from interiors to exteriors. You can see where your extra crowds are and when the stunts work. You can see your "**Story Days**," separated by the red lines, which you can later check with the script supervisor.

You can photocopy it, post it in the department as a guide and re-minder as to what your department is working to achieve. You can post it in the office or the truck on location to check against daily continuity. And you can use it to pull your next set of breakdown sheets.

The next set of breakdown sheets are called "**Cast Breakdown**" sheets and are for the people who need to be specifically costumed.

They are:

• Main Cast; these are the people whom the story is about.

• Secondary Cast; these people have large parts but appear less often, in cameo or featured running parts.

• Featured Bits; they may have only one line each but it's written and the camera will be on them so they form a part of the visual tapestry.

• Silent Bits; They may never have lines but are a featured part of a principal group (The drunk who falls down in the bar, a posse member or the silent group around the chief). They are distinguished by taking direction from the director instead of the second assistant director, as other background.

- The Stunt Players; sometimes forming a large part of the cast as in, "the bad guy's gang." Most often blending into the background and appearing as extras who get killed or sometimes only appearing as doubles for the cast.
- Background or atmosphere; List the various types of groups of people who would inhabit the background and populate the world that the story is set in.

The reason for this breakdown is to isolate the individual changes for the players so that they may be assessed, budgeted, accumulated, and kept track of through their work until the end of production; and to discover and list the amounts and types of background costumes needed.

This set of breakdown sheets will become "The Set Book" which will record the life of each major costume on the show and provide a guide for "matching" the continuity of an actor's change through a jumbled production schedule; they are usually notebook-size forms divided into three or four horizontal boxes, each box listing, in chronological order, the change number according to scene number of an actor's clothing ("**Joe Blow, Change #1, Scene Numbers 1-5, Int. Saloon, Day**" goes into the first box and a description of the change follows: "Change #1 — Black #1 hat w/silver band, black shirt and pants, tooled boots.")

This is done for every character and every change. If the change is repeated *exactly*, its scene number can go in the same box, but if the change is altered slightly for another segment it's given the same number with a letter reference, 1A, 1B, etc. Information such as "doubled for stunt," "gets wet," or "progressive aging" go in the appropriate box. Soon we can get a good sense of the amount of *necessary* costumes the show needs to shoot the main characters and their stories. From these character-change sheets, one can determine how many costumes the players will need, when they have to have multiples (for stunts, damage, excessive use) and help tell you whether the costumes will have to be made, purchased, or rented.

*During production, the day that the actor first works in that scene, the outfit is recorded on Polaroid or digital film (as it plays in the scene). The picture is filed in the set book, chronologically by scene and outfit number, with a brief description of how the clothes were worn (collar open, sleeves rolled up twice, etc.).

A permanent record is developed, scene by scene, change by change, actor by actor so that — in the event of retakes or matching clothing from "interior" to "exterior," shots at different times and/or locations, or changes of wardrobe personnel — one will always know who wears what and how it was worn.

Now's the time to look for "multiples." Multiples are figured in the event that one set of clothes for a given change is deemed insufficient. It's always a good idea to have at least doubles in shirts, ties, hats, and dresses for your cast just in case of sweat, make-up slip, lunch spill, or other un-foreseen disasters, or if your location is in place where overnight cleaning is impossible. In the event that your overall budget is small, this isn't always possible, but if the change works a lot, at least try to double the part that is seen closest on camera, usually the clothes surrounding the face.

Examples of other situations that demand doubles are:

Weather: Let's say that your cast member, "Bill" the sailor, works on the deck of a ship during a rainstorm in a long action sequence. Two or three complete changes for "Bill" and two or three for his stunt double may do it. In addition, the stunt double is a different size from the actor, and has to wear special shoes for the wet deck and oversized clothes to hide a wet suit underneath....

As you can see, this scene, while simple reading, will call for a lot of information, work, and money. Find out the cost of wetsuits, have a chat with the stunt coordinator about the scope of the stunt and sizes of the stunt man, then get ready to query the director about how the scene will be shot, because all the information that you acquire will be needed when you have a "money talk" with the line producer.

Location: If your shoot will be in and around a lot of water, streams, swamps, rainy areas, you can bet that your cast will get wet at some point. Extra footwear and socks, to complete extra changes, will be a consideration.

Stunts: Always a factor. Extra clothing for *stunt doubles.* Doubling actors should always be checked on with the stunt coordinator. Also, sometimes the stunt requires that the stunt person wear protective clothing, harnesses, or have fireproofing done — things that are not strictly thought

40

of as part of the "costume look" of a show and are sometimes overlooked until late in the preparation period, or on location, when the last thing you need is having to invent or acquire more costume elements.

Progressive Aging: Let's say that your characters are lost in the jungle for a period of time and we see them degenerate on screen. In the beginning, they look right out of the city; next, they look rumpled and a little soiled; next, they get dirty and start to get torn; last, they are in filthy rags. How many sets of doubles? Well, if there are four main stages to the aging, four sets might do it. If stunts are involved, then perhaps eight or more duplicates will be required.

★On *Rambo III*, I had almost 50 duplicates for Mr. Stallone, even though it was the same black "U" shirt and cargo pants every day. There were Mr. Stallone and three stunt doubles and the change worked every day for months, constantly being washed, over-dyed and repaired, to always look the same on camera.

Special Effects is a department that is required to be hard on clothes. Usually "squibs" (bullet hits), but "fire gags" and "water gags" are their province, also. They always want to have two or three garments available for them to destroy, per gag, apart from the changes you need to costume the show. On big effects productions this can run into the hundreds of garments. Here, after you realize the scale of destruction, you can determine whether it will be more cost efficient to manufacture, purchase, or rent the costumes you need to destroy.

Decoration and Property Department: Technically, when an actor removes his hat or coat in a scene it becomes an "Action Prop" and most prop people will inquire if you plan to have the described item there that day or not. Sometimes they will want to "hold" the item if it works the next day. I always keep principal wardrobe locked in my truck, on stage or in the department, but understand their concerns.

It's a good idea to check with the decorators as to whether they are planning on using any wardrobe for set dressing in closets, drawers, clothes lines, sites of the wrecks, or whatever. If the answer is "yes," I explain that I'm only bringing enough wardrobe to do the changes of the actors. If they need wardrobe, I will rent what they want (if I have time), put it on

41

separate rental sheets, and pass it on to them. I like decorators, and have decorated sets myself, but they will always use the clothes you give them with casual abandon, strewing them about rooms or hanging them on exterior clothes lines (in the rain, no matter). When they're done with them they will, sometimes, return them dirty, stuffed into boxes or paper bags. Please, spare yourself the agony and get them what they need, so as not to interfere with the costumes that are available to *you*, to do the job *you* have to do.

The next (and last) set of breakdowns has to do with "**Background.**" Going back to the "Chronology Breakdown" we can now pull a list of background requirements together.

When you read the script you have to read between the lines. In any dramatic presentation, the story concerns the cast playing out the drama, as they move through a series of locations, time, and background crowds. The question is, how are these crowds composed (size and type) and how much will it cost to do them? The scene says "Train station day." The key players meet on the platform, talk and walk away. When you read the scene, what do you see? If it's a "normal day" there might be 100 or more people there. Every script is different, but by now you should have a feel for the scale of your production. (At this stage, production people may not be available or the decisions about extra counts may not have been made.) Take your best guess. Call it 100, if you feel that's about right (you'll be able to change it later when there is more information from the production office). Now, list the 100 background people by type. What kind of people would be in a train station (what's going on in your story?). Let's say it's the Old West: 20 couples (better-dressed, day wear)... that's 40 people; 10 "train types" (conductors, red-caps); 10 soldiers on leave; 10 cowboys; five blanket Indians... that's 75; 10 Mexican types; five nuns, five salesmen in plaid suits; and five trappers in leathers. Okay that's 100 people with a little variety and Old West flavor. Now, do that for every set, keeping in mind what types would sell that period, location, mood, etc. When you're satisfied that you've accounted for most or all of the major types of costumes that you'll need on your show, then start a page for each group.

42

Page One, 10 Cowboys, w/15 Outfits for fittings.

> 15 Hats, Western character
> 15 Hat bands, asst., leather, horse hair
> 15 Bandannas, various print and plain, cotton, silk
> 15 Long John tops, over-dyed
> 15 Shirts, long sleeve, assorted
> 15 Vests, wool, assorted
> 5 Coats, wool, 4-button, asst.
> 5 Coats, outer, mackinaw, wool, assorted
> 15 pr. Suspenders
> 5 Belts, wide
> 15 pr. Pants, wool, cotton asst. top pocket
> 15 pr. Chaps, leather
> 15 pr. Cuffs, leather
> 15 pr. Boots, Western
> 15 Slickers, oilcloth, yellow
> 15 pr. Spurs

Page Two, 20 Women, Better Dressed - Day - 25 Outfits to fit.

> 25 Hats and prairie bonnets
> 25 Day Dresses – cotton, asst.
> 25 Shawls, silk
> 25 pr. Hose
> 25 Corsets, white, boned
> 25 Camisoles, white ctn. with ribbon trim
> 25 pr. Gloves, day
> 25 pr. Shoes, period, high-lace
> 25 sets "foundation" wear (as per dresses)

As you do this, you will find that you may not need shoes for every person in every crowd, only to cover your largest amount. You might want more hats than outfits, so the clothes become more versatile; black suits and dresses might work on both the funeral crowd and the train station atmosphere.

You will want to have an extra allowance of clothes over your crowd amount for "Fitting Stock" — at least 10%.

The schedule will have an effect on your count and budget. If several different large crowd scenes are scheduled on consecutive days, you will face having to have clothes available for pre-fitting tomorrow's crowd while today's crowd works in front of camera and yesterday's crowd needs a couple of days to be broken down, cleaned, and restocked. This means that the same clothes are not available for use every day and you may need clothes for every crowd mentioned. This is a situation that has to be solved with production and you will only find out after the First Assistant has made up the shooting schedule on his or her production board.

You will begin to see the clothes as units, building blocks that can be combined and re-combined to get the desired effect on each set, throughout the production.

With the completion of these breakdown pages you now have a group-by-group inventory list that you can discuss with the line producer for direct cost, as well as the amount of time and wardrobe labor necessary for preparation. You can talk to the director for ambiance, confer with the assistant director for atmosphere amounts, and look to your own department for the amounts and types of stock to be developed, with a built-in check list to ensure that nothing has been forgotten.

The next step is to assemble all this information into a comprehensive "Budget Package" — your Department Business Plan.

Apache man
Geronimo

USMC
Patrol
Jacket.

Steve Kanaly
The Wind and the Lion

chapter 8

THE
BUDGET PACKAGE

Producers contract to make a film project for "X" amount of dollars. The way they come by that figure has to do with the type of deal they have and the expected releasing pattern. Sometimes money is raised and the show budget is created later, by percentage — that means that each department is given a slice of the budget pie, not according to the realities of their departments' requirements but by formulae... and a "This is all your department has" mentality governs the show. Needless to say, this can be very frustrating when you start to develop a projection of what you think of as your "real" expected costs, only to find yourself "way over budget."

The only way to be able to have realistic budget discussions with producers and production managers is to have all your costs documented. If costs are more than they want to spend or have to spend, you will be able to arrive at compromises with them, relating to the production requirements written in the script. For this reason, a strong, insightful, and clear budget is demanded.

A long time ago a producer told me that no one ever did anyone a favor by turning in a budget that was too light (unrealistically optimistic), because if he had to get more money to finish the film, it would be the most expensive money he would ever get.... So, as my old Chinese grandfather used to say, "Things that come too cheap in the beginning, come too expensive in the end."

Your budget will be broken into three categories:
1. Costumes — the cost of acquisition.
2. Labor — The cost of all direct labor expense.
3. Department Overhead — everything else.

Once you have completely developed your breakdown sheets, you can price each group of costumes according to their points of origin (rentals, purchases, and/or manufacture).

At this point, you also have a basis for a discussion with any costume house in the world, as far as availability of stock, pricing, and constructing a package deal (of which more will be said later). You also can develop a shopping list for outside vendors and costume makers.

As you research the costs of acquiring the needed costumes for your show you will pencil in the cost numbers on the appropriate pages of your breakdown sheets, with totals at the bottom of each page. All of this can be done manually or by computer program.

Other items that will affect the amounts of clothes you need and your budget-thinking will be:

Comfort Clothing: For actors. Shooting at night or in cold weather or with water work? You need to build in a budget for towels, robes, warming jackets.

Second Unit and Schedule: "Second Units" are common on "action" films and composed mostly of stunt people and extras. This unit can greatly expand your department requirements for rentals and labor, especially if shot concurrently with first-unit principal photography, giving you two (or more) shooting companies to service at once.

Schedule information will help you schedule your department's labor and acquisition of costumes. You might find that you have more time for manufacture, if some clothes work later in the shooting schedule; but never plan too heavily around the shooting schedule... if they change their minds, you're in trouble.

Crew Requirements: Will you be required to have safety gear or protective clothing for the crew? Hats for the sun, waders for water work? Some companies understand weather or other conditions will necessitate a certain amount of company-provided crew wear and will have you put those items in the budget; other companies will not want to spend the money on these items. If the answer is "Yes," I always ask production to send a memo to each department head requesting what items they want and the sizes, then give these items over to the departments on a *one-time*

48

basis. If the answer is "No," then I ask production to publish a letter to the crew, informing them that the company will not be responsible for crew-needed items and that they have to provide their own. This heads off potential bad feelings later on; however there are times when unexpected weather hits or someone "forgets to bring" and you may be asked to run to the local store and get rain ponchos, boots, hats, etc. When this happens, remind production that this requirement should come from some place other than your wardrobe budget.

Research and Development: or "R&D," as it's called. This is money reserved to buy research, sample fabrics, to make or buy sample garments, to arrange for outside pattern making and grading, dye tests and materials, mold making, and the like. Things that contribute to your costume stock, but aren't part of it.

Dress Extras and Reenactors: Sometimes, producers engage the services of dress extras or reenactors (living-history folks). These are people whom the producer feels can wear their own, sometimes home-made, costumes in order to save money. While *sometimes*, their uniforms are worth using — they're almost always too clean and bright, and because they are personal, you can't age them — their civilian clothes are sometimes a little disappointing. Lacking in a unified color scheme and exhibiting every level of manufacture, you will lose control over the composition of background crowds unless you are able to bring as much background clothing as you can, at least key and character pieces.

I have worked many shows with reenactors and some of them have worn really great outfits, but not all of them. So, when I have this suggested to me I always ask if the producers, who are spending millions of dollars on this screen project, really want the "look" of the film left up to what an extra wears on any given day.

A cautionary note: Take nothing for granted with regard to the availability or cost of costumes. Research with phone calls, detailed descriptions, Polaroids and first-hand visits to costume rental houses *before* you commit to production that you can deliver a show for a price. If you're not convenient to a costume house, most, for a fee, will digitally photograph samples and email them to you. Never estimate what you think a costume house will charge you — call and find out. There's always a chance that what you need won't exist for rent. Large shows regularly manufacture, and/or purchase, great amounts of costumes at various costume houses. Almost every costume house has the means and contacts for providing any type of fabrication or purchase. They are always ready for a serious discussion about providing for your needs. If you send a copy of your breakdown sheets and copies of the relevant research to world-class costume rental houses, they will be able to talk to you about a bid for providing everything, or pieces, as needed. (See Chapter 14, Accumulating Costumes).

LABOR BUDGET:

Start with a piece of graph paper (or a computer spreadsheet).

Number down the left-hand margin as many jobs as you think you will have: **Designer; Assistant Designer; Supervisor; Lead Costumer; Key Set; Truck Person** (including day labor); **Aging Person; Dyer; Asst. Dyer** (manufacture labor); **Cutter; Stitcher; Milliner** (location help); **Laundry Person; Location Alternation Tailor;** etc.

You want to list any and all jobs that will be paid by your company's payroll and work directly for you. Do not include vendors, since they have already been accounted for in the **Cast** or **Background Manufacture** and **Purchase** part of your budget.

Now, estimate the preparation weeks necessary, travel time to location (in weeks), location shooting weeks, wrap weeks, return shipping time and final return period and assign one square per week across the paper from left to right, after the job positions. This budget page will look similar to your Crossplot.

The next thing is to figure who will work and how long. **Designer,** for example, might work the entire show, so put a slash in every square for "prep period, production period, and wrap period." The **Key Set Person** may only work one or two weeks of an eight-week prep, for the entire shooting period and then have no wrap time, so mark the appropriate squares.

This is where you really have to consider everything that may happen to your show, such as how much help you need to get the costumes together, how much set labor to work the shoot, how much of it is local, what kind of department capabilities are necessary on location? (Later we'll go over some things that might influence you or that you might want to take into consideration.) If preparing at a costume house, will your deal with them include any costume-house labor?

Now you have a series of time-period squares behind each job, each of them checked for the amount of weeks that each person is expected to work.

Somehow, arrive at the pay level for your show. This may be union scale, plus an overtime allowance, or a flat-rate allowance. Whatever it is, make it realistic; remember, you're not doing anybody a favor by submitting unrealistically low numbers out of fear or hope. Put the weekly pay amount in each square behind the correct job heading, run the numbers and you should have an estimate for the labor cost of your show, person-by-person, job-by-job, and phase-by-phase: preproduction, production, and postproduction.

★Check labor laws. A 1994 labor law states that people must be paid a regular, hourly wage for the first eight hours per day, or the first 40 hours per week (negotiable for non-union workers). After that, they must receive time-and-a-half (1.5 times the regular hourly wage), from 8 to 12 hours. After 12 hours per day, some states demand more time-and-a-half, while some states require "double-time." This means that a day consisting of 16 work hours (not uncommon on location) could equate to 22 "pay hours" at a straight-time rate. (8 hours at straight-time rate, 4 hours at 1.5 times straight-time rate, plus 4 hours at 2 times straight-time rate.) Remember also that a "fringe" package is added to the wage to cover social security and taxes (approximately +12%). In the case of union workers, the fringe package also includes vacation, holiday, and pension/medical (approximately +17%). You don't have to figure all this out, since the show accountant will know all the real costs. But, you should know the implications of your crew decisions and demands. Running a picture budget from the other side (producer side) is a very sobering experience, since *everything* costs more than it seems to, at first glance.

DEPARTMENT OVERHEAD:

Think down your outfits from head to toe: **Hats**, **Wearing Apparel**, **Shoes**... That's all there is. Now, after you assemble these items, how will you work with them? (And that means service them.)

You have to think about the department and the location conditions, and decide how best to provide for the physical space you need to work. On a large feature, it's not uncommon to have a central warehouse, or rooms at the local motel, feeding one truck or more, with a large tent on location to dress extras.

Once set up, the daily process will (almost always) be:
- The working clothes will travel to the set on a daily basis.
- Actors and extras will be fitted and dressed.
- Set operation through the shooting period.
- Daily maintenance/alterations.
- Clothes returned after shooting (never left in dressing rooms).
- Cleaning/pressing, most often overnight.
- Stock work in readying for the next day.

In addition, you will be doing alterations and possibly building costumes on location and have to provide for some scale of workroom set-up.

You will need some kind of provision for a bill-paying, recordkeeping, and research-storing, working office.

Before you can come up with a department-overhead budget, you have to assess the workload on your show and develop a list of purchases for the expendable supplies and equipment required by the work you have planned or foresee, taking into account each phase of department work.

Under the best of conditions, you will have a well-seasoned Supervisor to help plan this phase — but if you are working alone on a smaller production, you still have to think about it.

PREPARATION:
Office
Space at a costume house; rental warehouse; truck interior; home; general office supplies; computer; file box; paper supplies; copying capability; telephone/fax; cell phone/pager; office furniture; refrigerator; coffee-maker; lighting.

Department
Physical space for accumulating costumes; clothing pipe racks — rentals, home-built, purchased?

How much rack space do you need in your department, on your truck, in the extras tent?

Measure the clothes at a costume department or your closet. You can get about 100 shirts or dresses on one crammed six-foot rack and fewer overcoats. While that's fine for truck shipment, you can't work that way. You might only get 10 to 15 complete outfits to a six-foot rack or roughly, two, three or four outfits, complete and hung together to the running foot (depending on how voluminous the costumes) so, that's about 100 feet of rack for every 400 outfits, maybe twice that for the extras' dressing area, where people have to sit and change, side by side. If every extra is allowed a foot as his or her "closet" to hang clothes, then the number of rack feet equals the number of extras; for a six-inch allowance, half as much.

You'll need rolling racks (purchase or rental?) to shuttle the costumes about and you might decide that the whole department will be better, portable, on rolling racks.

Figuring the rack space needed to house your department, plus the rack space needed to dress extras might result in a lot of rolling racks, with their own storage problems.

All this differs with the number of location moves your department has, the number of extras you're required to dress and the size of the department you'll need to facilitate it all. Experience is the best teacher, but you can find people who have done it before and have answers or ideas as to the best way to proceed.

Prices for rental racks can be obtained from any costume house, while the cost for building semi-permanent racks can be calculated by calling around for the raw material prices. Schedule-40 galvanized pipe, in one-inch diameter, has always worked the best for me, with 2 x 4s and 3/4" C.D.X. plywood used for the up-rights and bracing. Sometimes the construction department can build racks, tables, and shelves for you, on location, but you have to organize this with Production first.

SUPPLIES:

Hangers. You'll need them every day. Plastic, wood, wire, clip, suit, dress? It's all personal preference.

And all the usual list items: Shipping tags (for clothing-size alteration instructions, daily notes); safety pins; pens (Sharpies, markers — they go fast); boxes; string; and other supplies that are dictated by work or set requirements. Some items might be: Plastic garment bags; plastic shoe bags; electric floor or hand steamer; iron; electric or manual hat stretcher; felt hat reducers.

I'm not going to try and list every type of supply available, since I have included a list of costume houses with supply stores in the back of the book.

On an average size movie-of-the-week (MOW), expendable supplies can run a few thousand dollars. On large features, several thousand.

WORKROOM:

If you have to set up a shop to do alterations and/or construct garments, you have to consider the following: What are you asking the garment makers to do? What level of skill and experience will it take? How many people will it take? Given the time and work load, what supplies will they need (sewing machines, hand tools, leather working equipment)? What will the shop have to look like in terms of furniture (cutting or work tables, lights)? What about raw material storage (shelving units, storage boxes)? What kind of space will it take to house that operation? Where will that space be located? Does it have enough natural light or will it need color-corrected fixtures (you don't want to make any decisions regarding color of materials or dyeing under neon or other non-corrected light sources.) How's the air? Need fans, air conditioning, heaters?

The answers might be simple or complex, cheap or very expensive, depending on your show... but now or at any other time, the questions and Workroom provisions are the same.

If you have a really big project or are inexperienced, you might try and sit with the people who will head up the Workroom and get their input.

I can tell you that on an MOW-size show where I've had two or three garment makers and/or alterations people, that shop cost between $500 and $1,000/week in supplies for every week it's up and running, and that's not counting large material purchases.

If you estimate a large or unexpected Workroom force you might be asked to justify it.

The reasons are these;

- **First**: No matter the show, there will always be some things that are not rentable, not buyable, not findable, but they are things that will contribute mightily to the look of the show. Your only option is to make them yourself, under your own control and supervision.

- **Second**: Alterations — Never in the history of filmmaking have all the cast been fitted and approved in costume before shooting. You are sure to get some, even most of your cast, a day or two before they work. How will you get them fitted? Who will do the on-site manufacture and alterations?

- **Third**: Equity — There will always be some loss and damage at the end of every show. Everything you make for yourself, like everything you buy for yourself, becomes a company asset. At the end of shooting you have developed stock that can be used to off-set some or all of your "loss and damage," (L/D), and maybe even make a profit.

In the end, a well-planned Workroom could pay for itself.

★Note: always have a secure space for Principal Costume "Lock-up."

AGING / WASHING / DYEING:

Again, this varies from show to show, but let's take them one at a time.

Aging: (Discussed on its own, in Chapter 17) This is usually a thing you run into in war or Western films, but it happens on smaller films in limited amounts with "character" clothing. However you choose to do it, it's labor intensive and uncertain. You have to allow yourself extra garments for mistakes. I've seen shows where full-time aging staffs of 10+ people labored for weeks to distress one group of costumes after another, using thousands of dollars of supplies.

Washing: This is a constant job for wardrobe — the only choice you have is how to do it. Department washer and dryer (more than one?), the local "Fluff and Fold," the local commercial laundry, a Laundromat, the washer at your location motel, your bathtub. Many a costumer has spent many an hour washing or dyeing clothes in the bathtub in the motel room, on location. (Make sure you clean the tub with bleach before you check out.)

Whichever combination you choose will have a dollar amount attached to it, plus the final show cleaning bill. You might guesstimate by using 15% of your costume budget.

55

Dyeing: Usually means "over-dyeing," but sometimes Designers like to dye fabrics themselves for certain costumes. Only you know for sure on your show, but every dye operation needs hot water... washing machine, hot plate, various pots and pans for fabric swatches. If you're going to do it or send it out, allow something.

SET OPERATIONS — SHOOTING:

Transportation

While not strictly part of the costume budget, on small shows, you are all working out of one pot, so you have to consider how your costumes are going to be moved around and warehoused. If it's wheels on roads, it's Transportation. I've also been on locations where the "tent camp" was provided by Transportation — this could be where your extras change. Even if these requirements don't come out of your budget they come out of Transpo's, so go over your requirements with them. By the way, many costume houses own ready-to-roll wardrobe trailers for rent.

Under transportation you might also consider "ground shipping." Going to order stuff from another state? Going to ship to another country? You might allow for UPS, or FedEx, for domestic shipping. But, if you're going out of the country, you will have to come up with estimates on shipping boxes (costs) with an estimate of how many you will need, their sizes, and what they will weigh when packed for a shipping company like Pac-Air.

SET SUPPLIES:

These supplies are sometimes supplied by costumers for a "kit rental" fee. If not, you'll have to supply people tools to work with, including: Scissors; pens; leather punches; a "Leatherman" tool and other small hand tools. In addition, you'll have some kind of camera, film, notebooks, Toupee tape, two-faced tape, Gaffer's tape, sewing kits, whatever they need to work the set with. I always used to give all my set people surplus military back packs. I found that they're a good answer to carrying stuff around while keeping your hands free.

WRAP:

Cleaning

Leather is the most expensive to clean, then wool, linen and last, cotton. Women's things tend to be more expensive than men's. Extra money to hand-spot make-up or blood stains. Speaking of blood stains, you can help yourself in the beginning by adding liquid soap to whatever blood is being used and soaking the garment right away after the action.

PACKING FOR THE RETURN:

By box, or hanging in a truck? What's your expense?

"L and D":

I always plug in 10% of my rental budget for eventual loss and damage. This includes items that have been destroyed during the course of filming and items that have been lost to theft or carelessness.

RESEARCH:

The next piece of information to add to your budget package is research. In reality, you start researching the period as soon as you know what the show is about, and it's the research that helps you develop the concept for both foreground and background. Years ago at Fox, the department head told me "I don't care what it is, if it's in the script I want to see a picture of it!"

Think about some kind of allowance to buy books, make copies, etc. There are various ways to do a research package but, like a résumé, "only show them what you want them to see" — that may be something to think about. After all, the old adage says: "Reality is the enemy of art." To be really helpful, research has to be very specific. I've seen people show photos of the wrong Indians or soldiers of the wrong period. Sometimes this can lead to situations that are embarrassing if confronted by someone on the production with the "right" research. Try to find images that show exactly what you're doing. You can always develop a costume concept that is at variance with reality, but you should know what the reality is.

- **First**: Historical, that is costume-reference books that show line drawings of the clothes.

- **Second**: Art book color photocopies that show how artists of the period saw themselves and their surroundings or how great illustrators depicted the period and, of course real photos, when available.

- **Third**: Textual, that is, printed regulations or historical, first-hand descriptions related to what we're going to shoot.

Check and see what the Art Department (including the property master) is using for research.

★I also have to admit, that as a costume-house employee, nothing amazes me more than costumers who come to search out clothes for their shows and aren't prepared with their own research. After all, it's *your* show, *you're* the one getting paid to do it. I've always thought it a little unprofessional to take a job, and then rely on a costume-house employee to do your show for you. On the other side, most costume houses employ certain people for their specific knowledge (military experts or period experts), and are happy to help you arrive at the best, most authentic, or realistic costumes available. But the bottom line is, be responsible, do your homework, ask questions, but don't dump your job on others — they might be wrong.

SKETCHES:
Allow something for art supplies. (See Chapter 12, Sketching).

SWATCHES:
These can usually be gotten for free, but it might take a few paid shopping days, sometimes a paid assistant.

★The accumulation of swatches is a great learning experience necessary to any Costumer or Designer. During the process of swatch accumulation you will discover new sources and fabrics (which can be an unexpected source of inspiration), while learning the availability of materials, prices, and the limitations of local sources.

Padding: This word has gotten a bad name. Building a financial "pad" into your budget is acceptable, although line producers hate the idea. They hate it because *They* pad the show budgets against cost overruns and don't want you to do the same thing. In making out any budget, there will be things that you don't anticipate. Adding a little padding to cushion you against additional requirements, cost overruns, or future budget cuts is prudent. You are not "hiding" money in your budget, you are estimating on the high side whenever possible, in order to be able to absorb escalating demands or price changes later; it's called a "silent contingency fund."

Well, it's a lot to think about... but it's always the same. Just put in the numbers that you think will be *reasonable*, and add them up on their own itemized page(s).

Combined with your breakdowns and budgets, research, and developed presentation material, you will have a complete reference tool that can help guide your department, by getting everyone on the same page (literally). This tool will quietly answer questions and settle disputes of historical accuracy, while giving you a sound basis (that may be updated) for discussions about money ("When we agreed on these figures, we were talking these numbers"), manufacturing, or escalating costs necessitated by production changes.

To recap, you now should have:

- **1) Actor Change Sheets**: a series of pages with every costume change described for every actor, noting multiples and the related prices with page totals.
- **2) Background Breakdown Sheets**: another series of pages, one for each type of background costume needed, with all the items described and priced with page totals.
- **3) Estimated Labor Cost Page**: showing the positions you feel you need to assemble, fit, maintain, and return the costumes from your department.
- **4) Department Overhead Cost Page**: itemizing expendables, supplies, and services, like outside cleaning.

(end of **Budget Detail**)

- **5) A Chronology Breakdown**: describing the script, sequence by sequence, with your guess on background types and amounts.
- **6) A Costume Crossplot**: on graph paper, (or computer spreadsheet) outlining the "show at a glance," giving you all the scene numbers and which actor works where.

• 7) **Research Package**: with photos, photocopies, Designer sketches showing the period, types of costumes historically worn and/or specifically designed, and swatches showing colors and fabrics that can be used and to what effect. (This package doesn't have to be submitted for budget reasons — but to show and gain approval from production).

The finishing page is the "Cover Page." List and number the pages with their page totals. Sub-total by groups. Add to "Bottom line" total. It should look something like this:

Page 1.	cast, **John**.	$ 1,000.00
Page 2-3.	cast, **Martha**	$ 10,000.00
	(sub-total, cast)	(**$ 11,000.00**)
Page 4.	**Townspeople, Men**	$ 40,000.00
Page 5.	**Townspeople, Women**	$ 70,000.00
Page 6.	**Police**	$ 5,000.00
	(sub-total, B.G.)	(**$115,000.00**)
Page 7.	**Labor Budget**	$ 50,000.00
Page 8.	**Department O'Head**	$ 12,000.00
	total rentals =	$126,000.00 Pages 1-6
	Show total =	**$188,000.00**

You can see that this gives you a well-designed budget tool for all the money meetings that follow. You can, at a glance, look up and explain each increment of your budget, pull out specific detail and adjust individual numbers. You can account for every expense that you anticipate and show on paper a clear plan for running and managing your show. It's a professional presentation that finds favor with the money types because it displays accountability and thoughtfulness.

If you do it correctly, it's hard to refute and helps you justify the money you need to do the job you all want to do. If production doesn't have the money you need and can justify, then they might have to agree to scale back on some of their requirements.

When hired on a new show and presented with an "Overall" budget amount, always ask "What does this cover?" If the answer is "Everything," then develop your own figures to reflect what you think your cost breakdown will be. I've never heard of anyone having too much money in the budget, but sometimes the money is really not there. If you back out the hard costs first — rentals, cleaning, supplies — you might find that you have no money for labor. My advice always would be to really consider not taking a show that can't afford you. You won't be able to do good work and it will turn into production-by-crisis — pressuring you into the temptation of not paying a vendor, or even trying to get friends to help you for little or no money. No matter, you'll be over budget anyway and lose friends and vendors, too.

But never say never... sometimes there's something about some low-budget idea that makes you want to try. An opportunity, a story well articulated, a location adventure, a friend's dream. In those cases, dive in, do your best, have fun, and sharpen your skills. There's nothing like a film-making adventure full of hard work and hopefulness. But, if you choose to accept the conditions, you have no cause to get disgruntled if it becomes something less than you expected.

One last thought. **Never, never, never**, use **your money, your checks** or **your credit cards** to finance department requirements, unless you're under an "Independent Contractor's" contract and plan to bill the company as a regular part of your business.

Of course, sometimes, "things" happen. When they do, remind production that **you** don't need more stuff — **they** do.

After you prepare budgets a few times and compare what you spent with what you thought you'd spend, you'll feel right at home doing the breakdowns and plugging in the numbers. You'll also realize that this paper groundwork is a foundation you'll need, time after time, for a successful department.

62

SCRIPT CHRONOLOGY

① SEQUENCE   PG. 1-7   SCNE 1-3

EXT. JUNGLE D. VIETNAM 1968

REILANDER (W/ 181 PATCH)
CORBETT
SANDERS
BUELL
DOERR (MEDIC)
ROTH (1ST SGT)
BVOMBERG (NEW GUY)
RICHARDS
HETHERLY
LEMANSKI
FAILE 4   (CAPT. CADRE-'TIGER STRIPES')

        COMBAT COMPANY IN FIELD - DIRTY/TORN.

+ 20-30 EXTRA SOLDIERS.

② EXT. SURVIVAL SCHOOL - HQ - DAY   (SCN #4 EST.)

    HUELETTE

        WALKS CAMP - 40-50 B.G. EXTRAS / CLEAN.

    INT. SURVIVAL SCHOOL HQ. - DAY   (SCN #5.)

        HUELETTE (SP.4)
        FALZAN (SP.4)
        ONETO (SFC.)

            JOKE ABOUT PET MONKEY (TO WEAR FATIGUES)
            W/ "SWADEBECK" NAME TAG.

            HUELETTE ASKS FOR NEW ASSIGNMENT

③ EXT. BOTTOM BURNED OUT HILL SCN #6

        REILANDER (COVERED W/ BLOOD)
        BVOMBERG (SHOT)
        BIG SOLDIER (SHOT)
    24 B.G. EXTRA SOLDIERS

        SOLDIERS ASSAULT HILL.

SCRIPT CHRONOLOGY

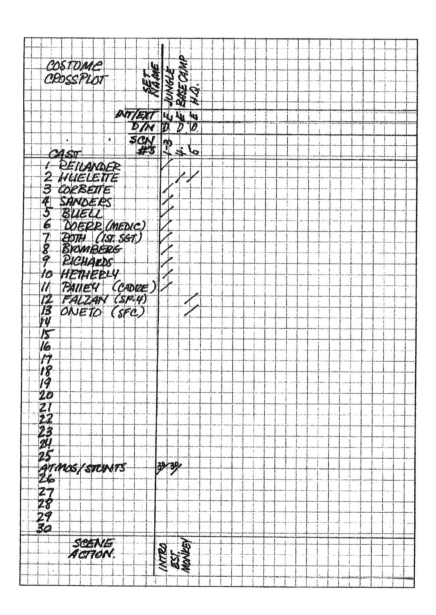

COSTUME CROSSPLOT

COSTUME FOR *REILANDER.*

Change	Scene Nos.	Set	Description
	1-3	EXT JUNGLE D.	COMBAT FATIGUES DIRTY-TORN.
	6-7	EXT HILL-BATTLE D.	
1.	8-9	MEDEVAC AREA D.	*BLOOD.
	10-11-12-14-15	INT. CHOPPER D.	
	16	BASE CAMP D.	
	17-18	BARRACKS D.	TPL'S THIS CHANGE.
	19-	LATRINE D.	NEW. FATIGUES -CUTS OFF NAME-
	22-25-26	I. HQ. D.	
2.	28	I. SURVIVAL SCHOOL D.	
	29	PARADE GROUND D.	
	30	BARRACKS D.	
	31	I. SUPPLY HUT. D.	(ISSUED TIGER STRIPES)
	34	EXT. SURVIVAL SCH. D.	(NEW 'TIGERSTRIPES') -NO NAME OR PATCHES
	35	I. MESS HALL N.	
3.	36	E. " " N.	
	38	I. E.M. CLUB. N.	
	40	E. E.M. CLUB. N.	
3A.	41.	I. BARRACKS N.	HALF DRESSED - RUNS OUT TO BUNKER.
	42.	E. " N.	
			T'SHIRT-PANTS-BOOTS-ONLY
3B	45-47-49	E. SURVIVAL SCH D.	FULL TIGERSTRIPES. W/All TAGS AND PATCHES SEWN ON
	51	I. MESS HALL D.	
	53	E. Survival SCH. D.	
	55	I. BASE ADMIN. D.	
	57.	½E SURVIVAL SCH D.	

ACTOR CHANGE SHEET

1.

Order Request

Purch shirt pants.

PRODUCTION CO.		DATE	8-31
SHOW NAME	LESSONS LEARNED.	DATE NEEDED -	
CONTACT		PO #	
PHONE		FAX NUMBER	

TYPE OF COSTUME
U.S. ARMY - INFANTRY - VIET NAM 1968 COMBAT COMPANY IN FIELD/AGED!

Amt	Consisting Of	In Stock	Unit Rental	Purch MO	Unit Cost	Total Cost	Total Rental
60	HELMET		10				600
60	LINER		15				900
60	HELMET COVER		10				600
60	CAMO BAND		5				300
150	'T' SHIRT, O.G.		7				1050
50	JUNGLE JACKET (MIX) 4P		50				2500
50	PANT TO MATCH (CARGO)		50				2500
50	BELTS- BLK WEB W/BRASS BUCK		10				500
100	SHOULDER PATCHES T.B.D.- SUBD			100			
50	BOOTS- JUNGLE- PANAMA TRED.		35				1750
50	HAT, BOONIE O.G.		25				1250
65	PIN ON RANK ASST. (3 EACH)		7				455
50	'U.S. ARMY' FLASHES SUBD.		3				150
50	NAME STRIPS - SUBD.		3				150
150	PR. BOOT SOX O.G.		7				1050
			@ 237				
							13,755

65

ORDER REQUEST FORM

DATE: PAGE 14.

SHOW TITLE :

POSITION	6 WEEKS PREP	6 WEEKS SHOOT	2 WEEKS WRAP	
DESIGNER	6@1000	6@$1500	1@1000	= $17,000
ASST	5@750	6@750	2@750	= 9,750
SUPERVISOR	5@1000	6@1250	—	= 12,500
SET#1	5@750	6@1000	2@750	= 11,250
SET#2	5@750	6@1000	2@750	= 11,250
TAILOR	4@750	6@1000		= 9,000
				$110,000 DIRECT
Costume house (@$35 hr. 1@40 hr-wk)	6x1400		2@1400 = $11,200	LABOR
LOCAL#1	1@600	6@750	1@600 = $5,700	
LOCAL#2 (LAUNDRY)	1@600	6@750	1@600 = $5,700	
			$11,400	LOCAL LABOR

DIRECT DEPT $110,000
COST. HOUSE $ 11,200
LOCAL LABOR $ 11,400
              $132,600

WARDROBE LABOR- SHOW TOTAL $132,600

BUDGET EXAMPLE.   5.

BUDGET EXAMPLE

BUDGET TOP SHEET

	Wardrobe total – rent/purchase	$ 52,340
	Department Overhead - supplies allow	$ 3,000
	15 shipping containers @$50	$ 750
	Cleaning/dying (@15% of rent/purch)	$ 7,851
	Department total – less labor	$ 56,090
Page # 14.	Department Labor	$132,600
	WARDROBE DEPARTMENT TOTAL -	$188,690

BUDGET TOP SHEET

LINDA
Kozlowski

Linda Kozlowski
Shaughnessy

chapter 9

COSTUME DESIGN

Okay, well that's over. Let's get to the part that you most likely bought the book for in the first place, **Costume Design**. (Refer to Chapter 1 for written guidelines.)

So, where do you start? You've read the script. Now you have to do a little noodling with a pencil.

Ask yourself a few questions: What kind of piece is it? Drama, comedy, action? What period is it? Is it an outdoor or indoor piece, or a little of each? What kind of action is there? What kind of mood is it? *What is the story about and who are the characters?*

These questions are important because the correct answers to them will lead you in the right direction in your costume selection.

Right here let me introduce you to two very different styles of costuming, "Documentary" and "Kabuki." The "Documentary" approach is obvious from the name and it's the safest because it's the most recognizable. You find out what was worn and reproduce it. Now that's never as easy as it sounds, but you always know what you're doing because of the historical research.

The other way, the "Kabuki" way, is more exciting, but if done incorrectly can be a disaster. The theory behind Kabuki is that, as you are doing something which never existed before anyway, why attempt to be literal? As the writer created a new reality by this drama, it is fitting that the visual presentation be free to illustrate that drama in a new way. In other words, create your own reality and if it's true to the drama, no one will question its correctness. This works for specific characters within a film, also, and probably works best on science fiction/fantasy films.

Actually a third way, the middle way, and perhaps the way in which most of us work, is a synthesis of those two — Staying loosely within a historical framework, while creating a visual that incorporates dramatic symbolism. Let's explore it a little.

You have to start developing a style somewhere in here. Some self-imposed rules that will help guide your selection process, based on what you want to accomplish — the **reasons** for your selections.

Go back to your show breakdown. You will see that the story takes place in location after location, through time.

Your main characters will travel from one end of the script to the other, through a series of scenes and sets, each having secondary characters and background atmosphere, a mood and time, living out the story.

Your job is to **illustrate** the drama with costumes so that the audience will accept the story via the visual construct. The costumes must support the dramatic premise of the piece in terms of their realism, integrity, and artfulness — and aid the actors by supporting and distinguishing their characters through their look.

When I went to film school at Pasadena Art Center, our instructor gave me a piece of advice that has proved itself, time after time. It goes like this:

> When, as a Designer, someone tells you, "I want this picture to look as real as possible," they most likely don't mean it, not in the historical sense, anyway; what they mean is, "I want this picture to be **acceptable** as real."

Which means, they want a good, professional illustration, not a bad school play. In other words, they want it true to character, but not always true to life; this understanding is the **very first step** in determining the level of illustration.

Metaphysically, you can look at it this way: All material existence is only symbolic of the invisible principles that have brought it into being.

Symbolism is the root of theatrical costume design. Costumes become metaphors for your characters' character. The clothes reflect the times, action, station, conditions, and even inner turmoil of your screen characters, while the background costumes create the world that your main characters populate.

The question is, how to create an effective illustration?

Start by looking at how others have done it.

See as many films as you can, new ones, old ones, ancient ones, foreign ones. See where the characters feel right and where the characters feel wrong. Where the background seems authentic or where it's "hokey."

Most films are populated with "stock" characters, that is, characters that we might meet in everyday life or everyday film life — the "doctor," "judge," "sheriff," "hooker," "housewife," "good-guy," "bad-guy," "love interest," "bum," "bartender," etc.

We've seen them so many times that these characters have become stereotypes. We recognize them at a glance. They have identifying looks all their own, and unless you're playing against type for a reason, it may be better to follow the ancient leads and try and create characters that are recognizable, but unique to your story.

This is truly where your job becomes exciting and challenging. To use the same general tools that have been used before, on the same types of characters that everyone's seen before, and come up with something that will stand alone as yours — while being at once understandable to an audience, supporting the dramatic premise, and helping the actors fashion character.

It's a lot but isn't as hard as it might seem. Everything that goes in front of the camera represents a series of selections, and every selection is done with a reason in mind. When you break down the script as a Designer (illustrator), you're discovering and developing the **reasons** that will enable you to make the **best** selections. Your reasons will become more refined as you develop more information (color theory, historical knowledge, language of symbolism) and your selections will become more refined, also.

When you read a script, you can picture it. Maybe the picture is a little foggy, a little unclear in detail.... What you need to do is organize your thoughts, analyze the requirements and find out what's available to work with.

The first place to start might be the question: "Why do people wear clothes?"

Historically, the first use of clothing was for protection from weather, then war, then modesty. No one can say where or when adornment started, but grave excavations have produced beads and shell disks that go back tens of thousands of years.

Egyptians were weaving linen and making gold jewelry six thousand years ago, and tribes people from the steppes of China were wearing decorated, felted clothing and woven plaids two thousand years before that. A ten-thousand-year-old "Ice Man," found frozen in the Italian Alps, was wearing a recognizable, fitted-leather shirt and pants with woven fiber sandals, and mummies from the Andes were found wrapped in woven woolen blankets with geometric designs.

Second: clothing was a display or reflection of rank (position), class (wealth), culture (ethnic-social-moral); and third: for beauty's sake, to feel and/or be attractive (even in a counter-culture sense).

The reasons don't change, the clothing does, with period, location, culture, conditions.

If you have to do a story about ancient China — a culture about which you may know nothing — with a little research as to styles and fabric, you know that the king will be fancier than the farmer. Ancient Egypt? The dancing girl will have less on than the merchant's wife, and so it goes.

Certain recognizable images of character appear: the self-absorbed "rich guy," the vain "other woman." We know the types, the characters, we know how **we think** they would see themselves, how they would express themselves with clothing. (The fun part is creating anew, or re-creating with symbolism in a fresh way, to tell your story uniquely.) In other words, we can grasp their self images as they are portrayed in the screenplay... but what, actually, would they wear?

Go to the visual research (this includes modern fashion).

When researching a period (or "look") there are only four things to look for:

• Silhouette

• Line (actual seams and cut)

• Detail (of construction, including fabric, trim, and jewelry)

• Color

Most periods are recognizable by their silhouettes and most people familiar with period clothes can spot the major changes by the size of the dress or length of the coat. Designing a futuristic show can also start with a concept of silhouette. What best reflects the character or conditions — sleek, heavy, layered, a lightly covered body or one shrouded to the point of concealment?

Within the silhouette is the Line and Detail: Is it draped or fitted, double or single breasted? Does it have bound edges? What's the fabric like — what's it made of and how was it made?

If the character is tedious, so might be the print of his or her tie or dress. Try and list the character traits of your cast, then translate them, symbolically, into costume, using cut, fabric, and color.

This is both the creative and interpretive part. In some scripts, a wild, clearly fantasy world is the background. In these cases you are free to invent a "look" that has nothing to do with reality and everything to do with symbols. But what about shows that are set in the past? Westerns or period dramas? Contemporary films? Audience members have seen things like this before and have preconceived ideas about what these films should look like. In these films you have to walk a fine line, making the costumes "realistic" enough to be accepted and not be distracting; while using your skills at illustration to highlight or underline characters and dramatic situations, sometimes with special bits of wardrobe called "signature pieces" — identifying pieces that reoccur on a character, sometimes with color. It all goes back to the same thing, what kind of illustration best fits your drama?

(The following is an excerpt from a print article I wrote for *Cineaste* Magazine, Spring 2004. It reads a little long but it sums things up.)

The main criticism that I hear is that Costume Designers tend to take too much historical "license." They alter what we "authentically" know about some historical situation, character or item of military equipage, and this alteration from strict historical fact makes the film somehow less than acceptable; it makes the film "Hollywood," "Fake," "Inauthentic," and by extension, makes the Costume Designer less than perfect. But is that criticism fair?

It might be if we worked in an industry where the mandate was to re-create the historical epoch down to every correct detail with no expense spared and as much time as was needed, but that's *never* the case!

In order to understand the job we have to explore the five major areas that shape the job and influence the outcome. They are: The Drama and its Characters, The Historical Setting, The Budget, The Collaboration, The Designer as an Artist.

1. The Drama and its Characters: The rules of drama haven't changed in about thirty-five hundred years: man against man, man against self, man against nature; protagonist vs. antagonist, hero — heroine — villain. These situations can be arranged into 20 master plots according to one book; a few more or less, according to others, but all drama is defined by/as conflict, usually with moral connotations; that makes every story a parable and every character a symbol for some condition or principle.

The real story then, resides not in the dialogue nor setting, but the theme, and the invisible Spirit of the film is revealed in its art-directed and costumed appearance.

The effectiveness of the communication relies on the strength and accuracy of the physical illustration, not of the superficial-quasi-historical appearance but of the character-symbols which articulate the theme.

Simply stated, this is why the "Good Guys" wear white hats and the "Bad Guys" wear black. It's no use saying "But that's not how they really looked." In a strict documentary one can be blissfully unconcerned with anything except research — but in a dramatic film, the point is to illustrate the drama so that the "Look" supports the premise; if you turned off the sound you could still recognize the genre, the parts and their condition — you may not understand completely but you would have a "pretty good idea" of what the story was about.

One way senior costumers would explain it to us was: "Suppose each scene was a book in itself and you were charged with drawing the cover illustration, something that would illustrate perfectly the *meaning* of the scene and its characters; in order to convey that information visually, how would you dress them?" John Milius used to tell me, "If you have a choice, always shoot the myth."

If you allow that a film is usually first an emotional document and only second, a historical document, then arguments about the relative historical non-accuracy of any piece become a little muted, less so if the costume in question serves the spiritual or thematic sense of the character better than the accurate one would have. In our business the characters, even historical ones, have to appear correct, even if they are in reality, inaccurate.

This search for the characters' significance is the first step for any Costume Designer, to identify the characters in the script by type and function. Once this is done the second step is to look at the story setting.

2. The Historical setting: Even a casual glance at research, while considering your prospects for re-creating a period, reveals a central truth: everyone and everything is a product of his, her or its own time; and although the clothes were what they were, they may not, for various reasons, be suitable for film costumes.

The reality of the past is the reality of the past, however, every attempt at a new re-creation is inexorably tied to the aesthetics of the period of translation, even more than the period being translated. Why? Because we live in the "now," and films are supposed to connect with a "now" audience. "Now" sensibilities are *always* going to intrude themselves. (This goes for editing and shooting styles, also).

By sensibilities I mean, not only popular taste, but the existence of certain textiles, trimmings, animal products, dyes, even craftspeople that would be necessary to accurately reproduce a distant period.

By way of example let's look at the three films about Cleopatra. The first one was made in 1917 with Theda Bara. It was obviously well researched, and everything — sets and costumes — were made-to-order.

75

In the late 1920s, the opening of King Tut's tomb set off a world-wide enthusiasm for all things Egyptian (so strong an interest, in fact, that it started the Art Deco movement). That, and the invention of sound, urged a remake staring Claudette Colbert in 1934, touted at the time as being highly authentic.

In 1963, Fox tried it again with Elizabeth Taylor. Now, all three films had the same characters, the same general settings, and access to the same general research. Why don't they look the same? Ancient Egypt didn't change, ancient Rome didn't change.

They look different because each film translated ancient Egypt for its own time and audience, with its own sensibilities and with the technology and materials available to it; and so it is with us.

The films we work on now with all earnestness, may appear to future audiences to be dated, not to the ancient past, but to US, because of our "Now" sensibilities, which we unconsciously build into them.

3. Budget: Unfortunately, admit it or not, this is the mother of all opportunities and all problems in doing any historical film; the direct influence of budget on the "Look" of the film cannot be overstated.

It doesn't matter — not the quality of your research, not your personal dedication to doing the most accurate portrayal ever attempted — what matters is what you can afford.

This is the difference between the look of a movie-of-the-week and a major studio film. Budget/money translates into preparation time, additional labor, purchases, rentals, and manufacture. Without time and manufacture dollars you have to rely on what's available for rent and in-stead of being able to create your film according to the look and feel you want, you have to shoe-horn your requirements into what other people have already made for other films (perhaps long ago). This is mostly successful on Westerns or other small films of a Victorian nature, and some military films, owing to the number of these films that have been made and the amounts of such stock still available for rent. Even so, sometimes you can be out of luck. That's when you have to be extra resourceful.

Working at various budget levels sharpens your aim. You come to realize that to get the most on the screen, in terms of quantity and quality, you have to prioritize your requirements and allocate your resources according to an organized plan of action that will make the best use of your budget dollar. This skill is no less important than researching a period or being a committed artist, in terms of doing the most effective job you can as Costume Designer. So, business sense is also part of the job of Costume Designer on any historic film.

Everything so far has been about the physical job requirements, but it is a people business.

4. Collaboration: This is by far the most difficult part of the job. I remember Sylvester Stallone once said to me, "If this movie comes out and it's bad, they're not going to say that the director made a bad movie or that *you* made a bad movie, they're going to say that *Sylvester Stallone* made a bad movie, so if I'm going to get the rap for it, I'm going to have things *my way!*"

What could I say, he was right.

The role of Costume Designer on *any* film can be, at the personal interaction level, potentially contentious, to say the least.

We are all hired technicians who bring our skills to a film and, in return, we get a paycheck and a screen credit. As Costume Designer I would like to feel that I'm the one who knows about the costumes and how to use them. I feel that as long as I'm getting the screen credit for the job I should be the one doing it, and I feel that if I'm the one running the Costume Department and the one responsible for its effectiveness, then production's requirements should go through me so that I can find solutions using the resources of my department. But what if other members of the production team don't see things that way and aren't the least bit concerned with my feelings about it? (Which, by the way, is sometimes the case.)

We work for the Producers. We help the Director with his or her film. We are expected to take the advice of the Production Designer and the Technical Advisor. We are the ones who help make the actors comfortable and beautiful, while working within the financial parameters of the accounting department and Unit Manager. We must orchestrate our colors with the Cinematographer, our materials with the Sound department, adapt costumes to the needs of Stunt personnel and reorganize ourselves at the instant insistence of an Assistant Director... this means that we can only intermittently do our job as we see it. The rest of our time is consumed by navigating the reefs and shoals of changing production requirements and bruised egos, and cross-purposing other departments' responsibilities.

There's no crying about it, it's the reality of filmmaking.

5. The Costume Designer as an Individual Artist: A lot of what anyone sees on screen is the product of the Costume Designer's imagination. Even with all the extraneous challenges, we are, after all, the ones who get the costumes — our ideas come through, overall, if not in every specific costume.

The pulling of rental stock sounds easy but it takes experienced attention to detail of type, size, texture, and color. Remember, there's no rehearsal for wardrobe crowds; clothing collected from many sources is combined on the day it works into complete costumes on background crowds — crowds that form believable backgrounds and atmosphere for the story to take place against.

Manufacture is where a Costume Designer is supposed to shine. Familiarity with color theory, textiles, their properties, drapery and usage, dyeing, various types of manufacture and designing garments for both looks and construction are the very essence of the job. Frequently, Designers are also great sketch artists able to create renderings that, once swatched, can be budgeted and translated into cloth by the experienced hands of the workroom.

With good Designers, the artistic dimension goes deep — they see the finished film in their mind's eye and work with their knowledge and resources to bring it into material existence, one garment at a time.

All the manufacture has to be done with an eye to how it will eventually fit into the overall presentation of the film and this may necessitate both large-scale manufacture and subsequent large-scale breaking down and distressing.

In the end, there's no doubt that nothing gains confidence like experience and ability, but that experience and ability have to be presented in a way that is helpful and non-threatening, and herein lies the real art of the successful Costume Designer: not only to have the right ideas that speak to universal understanding in the translation of history, drama and character, but the ability to present these ideas in a manner that sparks everyone's confidence and makes them desired by the other members of the production staff, including the cast.

So, the answer to the question, "What is the role of a Costume Designer on a historic film" might be: Historian, Artist, Craftsperson, Department C.E.O. and, perhaps most important, Diplomat.

MANUFACTURING COSTUMES:

With regard to the shape of the clothes, it all starts with the cutting. Where are the control darts? How tight is the arm hole? Period clothes arrive at their distinctiveness by their cut (and fabric), so you have to do some studying as to the historical progression of clothing. Remember, the more you choose to compromise the cut of period costumes for the sake of actors' comfort or as a concession to modern fashion sensibilities, the farther you will get from the look of the period.

FABRIC:

While you have many choices, you can break them down into categories that will make the selection process easier. Let's start with the two easiest to recognize: **light absorbent** and **light reflective**. Most natural fabrics are light absorbent, except for silk and, to a degree, polished cotton and linen. Most man-made fabrics are light reflective — Rayon, Nylon, Satin, Polyester.

Light-reflective materials can look elegant (as in a woman wearing a silk dress in a room full of black tuxedos), or, because of their shine, can look cheap, if overused. In period clothing, it translates into the lower-class wearing light absorbent (dull), and the upper-class wearing light reflective (silks with gold or silver and fur trim). Or, in a modern sense, the gangster wearing a shiny silk suit, the sober judge wearing a gray wool matte-finish. Or, the wife wearing a simple black dress, while the hooker is obvious in gold lamé shorts and vinyl boots. The simple cowboy wears a dirt-colored vest while the gambler wears silk brocade.

The more honest and "down-to-earth," the more light absorbent. The more wealthy or posturing as wealthy, the more light reflective.

While we're discussing the elements of costume design and things that will influence your decision-making process this might be a good place to hear from Captain Dale Dye – industry-famous technical advisor.

WARDROBE FOR WARRIORS
Capt. Dale Dye USMC (Ret.)

Given the industry's penchant for high drama, it's virtually inevitable that at some point during your career as a Designer or dresser you'll be called on to work on a war movie or military-themed project for one media or another. War and the attendant combat involved in prosecuting it has always been productive fodder for film and TV projects. You can verify that simply by reviewing the genre over the last couple of decades, or you can think about it as a storyteller does. And that's what you should do in order to bring your costume expertise to bear on a military project.

Ernest Hemingway, no lightweight in the storytelling arena, once said war is man's greatest adventure. That may be a little glib but it's also absolutely true in terms of human drama. No other genre in our business offers such an opportunity to examine and demonstrate the full gamut of human emotions. When lives are at stake and death is a very real possibility as it is in combat, people will at some point experience fear, rage, exhilaration, joy, mirth, pride, depression, tension, heartbreak and various admixtures of those feelings as a matter of course. Say what you will about the futility of it all, preserve your right to call it cruel, inhumane and politically motivated, but don't lose sight of the fact that it makes for great entertainment. It does and that means you should be anxious to work on a war or military-themed project when the opportunity arises.

But what can you bring to the table as a Designer or Costumer? These military folks wear uniforms and that means by definition that they are all meant to look the same. Uniform: One shape, one appearance, one look, so wouldn't it be a little boring, a little lock-step and simplistic? You can't just sit down at the drawing board and fantasize a uniform that includes cool patterns, vivid colors and dramatic flourishes. There are regulations that govern these things and no one is going to buy a soldier, sailor, airman or Marine that looks dramatically different from what audiences see in books, newspapers, and documentaries. Unfortunately, too many Designers ponder that for a minute or two after they've read a script, shrug and then pick up the phone to call the costume supplier and order up a selection of whatever uniform is appropriate, complete with boots, hats and helmets for both the bad guys and the good guys in the story.

Let the Props Department individualize the characters by giving them different weapons or equipment. That's that, roll cameras and where's craft services?

You can do it that way, but you'll be missing one of the most challenging and rewarding creative experiences available in our industry. Do a little simple research and you'll see plenty of visual evidence that uniforms may be designed to make military people look identical at the outset but that similarity rapidly disappears with the pragmatic concerns of survival and comfort in combat or a field environment where everyone is living rough. So, just copy the pictures? Select a look that's cool for a given character and make his wardrobe match the research. Done... and when's lunch?

Not done if you want to truly exercise your creative expertise. In fact, you're far from it. You need to understand why military people make modifications and how they do it to truly depart from the norm and lift your design contributions out of the ordinary. Most Designers and Costumers have no personal military – much less combat – experience and it seems counter-productive to enlist and spend three or four years out of the showbiz loop just to get it. So how can they get that insight, that creative edge?

Enter the Military Advisor. In the past 20 years or so, producers and directors have recognized the need to employ a person who has first-hand military and/or combat experience to advise them on story, look, and feel in military projects and in many cases train actors how to wear *your* wardrobe, while portraying real soldiers, sailors, airmen or Marines. This person can – and should – be the handiest, most effective tool in your kit but you've got to learn to use it. Build a solid, mutually respectful and trusting relationship with the Military Advisor and you've got an asset that can not only guide you reliably in costume matters but you've also gained a source that will stimulate your own creative efforts by explaining the realistic options you have... and don't have... in costume design for a military project.

But wait just a minute here. You mean to say this guy or gal gets the final say in costume design for a military project? Isn't that the Directors prerogative? I'm the Costume Designer and it's my job to help create characterizations via wardrobe and assist the Director and actors in bringing their visions to the screen. And if they are not interested or just don't know, isn't the look of the main characters and extras my responsibility as the Designer or Costumer? Who's in charge here?

81

The direct answer is you are. And you'll do just fine if you remember that good moviemaking is a symbiotic process and no one has all the answers or a monopoly on good ideas.

It's hard to be humble when you've got all the background, experience, and education in showbiz costume design, but you should start by making simple overtures when you discover a Military Advisor has been hired on your project. He's actually worn the uniforms involved in war and peace, so be willing to admit he might know a thing or two about them and likely has more detailed knowledge about accoutrements and options than you can find in any book or technical manual. Consult with your Military Advisor as early as possible in the design process. He or she will know what uniforms, patches, accoutrements, and frills you absolutely need, as well as those that can be eliminated when the budget numbers start to be crunched.

And he or she can show you some short-cuts or techniques for wear and care of uniforms that will make your off-screen life much easier and the look of your characters much more realistic. Bring the Military Advisor into your department as a trusted and desirable member of the wardrobe team. Avoid the attitude that you know best and all you need the Military Advisor to do is show you which ribbon or qualification badge goes where on what uniform. If that's all you're willing to give, that's all you're likely to get… until the Military Advisor calls a halt to filming and tells the Director that the uniforms he's filming are all screwed up. You don't want that.

Very often the look of military uniforms worn in combat or garrison has more to do with how the wardrobe is worn than what it is. That's where the Military Advisor can really help you – and particularly your dressers and on-set assistants – in a big and very important way. A performer needs to feel comfortable in your wardrobe. He or she needs to feel confident that the look is right when the cameras roll and there are more pressing issues – like acting – to worry about. The Military Advisor should be called on to work directly with your performers when they are being fitted to show them – and you – how a uniform item such as a cap is worn to get a credible look. There are valuable tricks of the trade (the Military Advisor's and yours) that are revealed when you do this and they pay lasting dividends throughout the shooting schedule. An example or two here might be instructive.

Take the beret as a classic item of military clothing that is more often worn incorrectly than not and tends to make the performer wearing it look both goofy and decidedly unmilitary. Real military people who carefully and lovingly modify, soak, shape, and wear their berets with a rakish tilt either laugh out loud or cringe when they see an actor on screen wearing something that looks like a misshapen pizza plate on his head. What happens leading up to this travesty is that the performer gives the costumer his hat size during pre-fittings and a beret is ordered from the costume supplier in that size. The beret, fresh from the manufacturer, is then slapped on the performer's head, pulled down on one side and we're off to the races with the actor looking like a refugee from a French period piece more than a squared away soldier. Had the Military Advisor been consulted, he or she would have told you that the beret is designed to be ordered smaller than the standard hat size, trimmed, soaked in hot water and then shaped on the head while wet to give it the proper look. You don't need to be an expert to immediately see the difference in the result on screen.

Then there's the business of blousing trousers over combat boots. You can go the easy route and simply stuff the trousers into the boots, pulling up a little slack and be done with it. That gives you the constant headache of having to check before each take to insure the trousers haven't pulled out of the boot-tops or showing either too much blouse or too little every time the actor moves, sits or stands. Understand that people are faced with this problem every day of a life lived in uniform and you'll figure they must have hit on a workable solution. And they have. Just ask the Military Advisor and he'll introduce you to inexpensive and readily available items like blousing bands that expand, contract and keep the trouser blouse nearly always perfect. It's no budget buster to get a hundred pairs of these little elastic bands or make them out of thick rubber bands if money and/or time is tight – and you've solved an aggravating wardrobe problem.

Most Military Advisors are proud of their service and want to see the people portraying them and their buddies on screen look right, but they understand it can't all be pristine and lock-step. They know from personal experience that military people more often than not make "field expedient" modifications to their uniforms in combat. They also know that such modifications are rarely – if ever – made in peacetime environments where looking sharp and regulation is a requirement. They can tell you what's right or plausible for any given situation; they can give you working parameters that keep you on a credible track, but you've got to solicit that advice and listen when it's given. Be personable, ask questions and let the Military Advisor be a part of your creative process. You'll save time, money, and frustration.

And let your dressers and subordinates know that the Military Advisor is your friend and is there to help. When you get into huge extra calls, let the Military Advisor inspect your uniformed performers before they wander onto the set. He or she is used to uniform inspections and can do them quickly and efficiently, making adjustments on the spot and saving you aggravation and mistakes that can lead to costly re-shoots or embarrassing edits.

Once the preproduction design, fitting, and modification work is done in the wardrobe department, many costumers are shocked to discover that their lovingly prepared uniforms are now about to be worn into a period of intense field training under the guidance of the Military Advisor and his assistants. Panic ensues. All that prep work might go down the drain with actors out in the jungle or woods crashing around in costumes designed for camera. Or – and this is the way you should be thinking about it – that field training/boot camp/rehearsal period will help you get the look right. Uniforms will be returned to you looking exactly the way real uniforms worn by real soldiers in a really stressful environment *should* look. You use those outfits as templates for aging or distressing and you can't go far wrong. More importantly, these periods of intense military training for the performers in your project quickly and accurately point to problems with fittings and durability, especially in boots and other footwear, which can give you problems during filming. Despite the isolation involved when they are conducting performer training, most Military Advisors are happy to have you conduct regular checks with them to spot and solve problems before they become disruptive issues for either the Director or the performers who have to wear your wardrobe.

Of course, this is all simply skimming the surface regarding the benefits that a trusting, give-and-take relationship with a Military Advisor can bring to your efforts as a Designer or Costumer. Military people are taught to look at the Big Picture. They understand synergism and believe in teamwork. The more you ask for their help and trust their advice, the more they are willing to give. In such ways wars are won… and great war movies are made.

JAPANESE SOLDIERS · SCN #919 (LAST STAND)

OFFICER

HEAD BAND

SWORD TIE

Ribbon BAR

WHITE KNIT GLOVES

LEAD SOLDIER W/FLAG

ALL TROOPS W/CAMO LEAFAGE

Japanese Soldiers prepare for 'Banzai' attack.

Dress
Upholstery
or mixed
textiles
'Kimono' shape.

Plastic scanned
over.
Moss hair
like real
down rock

SOFT FOAM ← seaweed new

R. laMotte.

Character, "Sea Witch," *Goonies* music video
(played by Cindy Lauper's mother).

chapter **10**

SPECIALTY
COSTUMES

GAG OUTFITS:

Almost every film contains some kind of "Gag Outfit." A "Gag" character outfit is one that is slightly exaggerated; one that you have to make up with the special purpose of setting a character apart, in something other than regular clothes. But, the end result is that it looks **almost** real — possible, but hard to imagine. Gag outfits come in two types. The first is the "Character" gag outfit, which might be the town drunk in a Western. Let's say you have that character in your script and don't know what to do to sell the outfit. Just putting him in regular clothing wouldn't do it; he would look like everybody else. You feel you have to do something special, but what? Then, you see an old silent comedy (the best repository for character gag outfits, ever) and see a drunk come out of a bar. The silent drunk is denoted visually, by his attached shirt collar, loose at one side, sticking up along side his ear, and, his starched shirt bosom, free and rolled up his front, showing under an open vest. You recognize him immediately and laugh at the cleverness of those long ago costumers who knew how to create character with costume.

The other kind of "Gag" outfit is one that "works" as per the script.

In *Goonies*, there was a child character who was an inventor. His inventions were always going a little bit wrong. In one scene, to scare the bad guys, he wore inflatable "muscles" that "puffed" him up when he pulled a CO-2 bottle string. We had to make a change for him that would look like the costume he wore in the rest of the film, but would expand on cue. The back of his clothes were made with spandex inserts. Custom-made balloons were attached under his clothing, and hooked up to feed lines connected to large bottles of compressed air, whose valves were controlled by an effects man. The whole rig was very difficult for him to put on and off because of the inside rigging, but in the end, it worked fine.

In *Curse of The Pink Panther* there were many gags, but the one that I remember having fun with was supposed to be on an airplane: as the Inspector walked down the aisle, his watch caught in the turban of a seated Indian passenger, and as the Inspector walked away to the bathroom, the turban unwound off the Indian's head.

We made a sewn down turban on a felt hat blank, bringing it up in a dome shape. We then coiled 30 feet of turban wrapping inside the dome, with the first couple of wraps on the outside. It looked great when it unraveled.

Burn Gags: This consists of the stunt person being set on fire. This is the most dangerous of stunts and no one will want to see anyone get hurt here. If you have a burn gag in your show, be sure to discuss this with the stunt coordinator, ahead of time. Costume doubles may have to be fire-proofed ahead of time. The stunt coordinator may want to avoid outer garments, made of synthetic fibers that melt.

Dancers: Shows with dance sequences require a lot of planning and often special construction, gusseted clothing, stretch material, special footwear, dance tails sewn in shirts and blouses, sweat shields, multiple clothing, fitted alterations, the list goes on. Check with the choreographer right away!

Children: Kids can be hard on clothes — they lose clothing, play between takes, and get things dirty. They work under special laws that govern time off and school, and, yes, many have "stage mothers" who will want to change the outfits. You have to assign a costumer to them.

Native American: Some are *very* touchy about how Hollywood, generally, incorrectly portrays them. Have impeccable research and *never* use real eagle feathers. First, they are sacred and can't be touched by females, including costumers, and second, they are illegal and can cost you a hefty fine ($10,000.00)

In a way, any characters who stand out are in "Gag" outfits and this might go for their clothes, their manner of wearing the clothes, or the condition of the clothes. I always look for opportunities to use a little "gag" piece, especially on "bit parts." The old character hat on the cab driver who has a line with the leading actor; the "salty" cardigan sweater on "Grandpa."

It's in the nature of creating character and by so doing, creating a more interesting and real world for the leading actors to inhabit. It's also an area that can be a lot of fun to work with, most especially the "treasure hunt" aspect. Visually, it separates the normal-looking film from the great.

SUMMARY:

A person can learn a lot about clothing, clothing manufacture, textiles, cutting, and sewing from any one of a number of "fashion schools" or "fashion and design courses." But, that's not really what Motion Picture Costume Design is about. Motion Picture Costume Design is about creating mythic images, revealing character, and illustrating drama using the principles of art and symbolism, as applied to physical clothing (which connotes a strong relationship to drawing and painting and their rules of composition, proportion, and color usage). When "clothing" is used as a means of artistic expression and dramatic insight, not an end in itself, but a descriptive representation in cloth for the character who wears it, it becomes a "Costume."

Blues
concept

chapter **11**

COLOR THEORY

Another consideration that will help you make decisions about the costumes will be color. Overall color and specific color.

How will you use it?

Again, while there are hundreds of hues (colors), and shades and tones thereof, there are only two color schemes possible: Complementary and Analogous. Get yourself a color-wheel at an art store. The way a color-wheel is arranged makes it easy to understand the difference: Analogous color harmonies are colors that sit next to each other on the wheel and are more sympathetic to each other, while Complementary harmonies are across the wheel from each other and offer more contrast.

In addition to colors, you also have black and white.

Now, how to best use that color depends on the specific nature of your project and the drama you're going to try and illustrate, but there are a few generally successful theories.

First, a few terms:

Monochromatic: This is a word that is frequently used and misused in production meetings by production designers and others. Monochromatic (color scheme) means: single color with various tonal values. In other words, eight shades of oatmeal.

My experience is that a lot of production designers are afraid of color overuse in the finished film or afraid that the costume person isn't capable of using color with restraint, and so, they favor "monochromatic" — but, is that what they really want?

In the '70s, when I first started hearing that term, some Westerns were done in monochrome, that is, everything was over-dyed with "tan" and became values of brown.

Today, when I hear that term, it usually means that a full-color pallet is acceptable if the various colors are mitigated and sympathetic in tone, with no "hot" color spots to distract the eye.

The answer may be a combination of bleaching and/or over-dyeing to create attractive, but muted, color combinations. Period shows, Westerns, dark dramas, can be darker and more single-value but still have a full-color pallet.

The necessity and importance of color requires that you learn color terms and usage from art instruction books on color theory. This is because "art books" use and explain the standard terms; and they will be the same terms that the production designer will be familiar with. Remember, everything you do is going to be filmed and displayed, much like a "Moving Painting." The director of photography (DP), the production designer, the key electrician, the set painters and scenic artists, all think and work with this in mind – you should, too.

You should learn to think about color in percentage values. Let's say you take a card — paint it white at one end and black at the other, then divided the space in between with eight (or nine) equal steps of gray. Going from white (0) to black (10) you would have created a "Gray scale." Now, where does your color value fall?

If I said, "Let's keep all our color around 50% or darker," would you understand? The production designer would.

If you were told, "over-dye everything with tan, that will mute the colors and bring them into the same range," would you understand?

First, "color" means just that, a color we recognize.

Hue is the name of the color. If you take red and tint it with white, you will get the hue of pink. Hue refers to the position of a color along the color spectrum.

Saturation, chroma, intensity: refers to the purity and clarity of a color – if you over-dye a bright yellow dress with a tan to "take it down," you de-saturate the yellow color.

Value: is the usual term for the lightness or darkness of a hue as it moves up or down a tonal scale (Gray Scale).

Tint and **Shade** refer to the use of white or black to move a hue up or down the tonal scale, making it lighter or darker. A color with white added is a tint and a color with black added is called a shade.

Warm and **Cool** refer to the tendency of a color to lean toward either the blues or the reds.

You also might want to study painters of the two color schools: "Colorist and Tonalist." The basic difference is: both schools felt that the impact of a painting rested in the tension created by contrast; Tonalists did it with subtle pallets, using tones and values of largely analogous schemes; Colorists did it by using primary pallets of bright color, often with complementary schemes.

With color usage rules and film sensibilities in mind, a "safe" costume pull might start monochromatic (medium analogous) neutral and natural; that is, medium brown (warm) or gray (cool) as a general background color... with off-whites (tan dip, warm, or gray dip, cool) and dark browns (warm) or dark blues (cool), set off with black.

The next colors to introduce might be: dark purple, mull, dull reds, dark earthy greens and "dirty" or dark yellows and oranges. Even with a restricted pallet, you can get "life" out of your characters. You can use Analogous color in the background costumes and Complementary schemes on the main characters.

My mother once told me, "If you want to do a beautiful period show, go look at the colors at the produce counter, and if you're doing a musical, look in a flower shop."

It's true, if the subject of your project is happy, sunny innocent, then the colors have to support it. If your mood or character is dark, cold, then the colors have to reflect that. If your subject is ancient or ethnic, then the dye colors have to be softer and more natural. If modern, the dye color harder, more aniline.

Remember also, all hues (colors) can be either "warm" or "cool." Red, considered a "warm" color, can be "cooled" by the introduction of a little blue; the reverse is true, also. Sometimes using two shades of the same color together can look terrible, usually because one is "warmer" or "cooler" than the other. In the '70s, some fabrics were printed using warm and cool shades of the same color, together, to get a contrast print (think paisleys).

93

The cut is historical and reflects the period, the color is emotional and reflects the mood, the fabric is textural and reflects station. What's the quickest visual way to tell a city person and a country person apart? A slick suit versus rough work clothes.

Again, you have to conceive of yourself as an artist whose job it is to illustrate a character, a drama, a mood, a period, a social condition. Your tools are: Period reference, hanging stock, workroom, fabric, dye, trimmings, department organization, imagination, and artistic knowledge... and some money from the producer.

Of course, everything you do will be aimed at the end result of being photographed on film, so it might be good to talk a little about the process of photography and what effect it has on the clothes.

Before you can photograph anything you have to light it... and it's this element, the lighting, that is important to understand because, it too, has to do with the mood of the drama and how it affects your color choices.

For anything recorded on film, there are only four lighting plots possible; they are: **High Key/High Contrast, High Key/Low Contrast, Low Key/High Contrast, Low Key/Low Contrast.**

High Key/High Contrast: The "Key" light is the main light, lighting the set. **High Key** light, might be the sun.

Contrast means the amount of shadow or the balance of light between highlight and shadow.

High Key/High Contrast might be natural sunlight with no bounce or secondary light to soften the shadows. The overall light is hot and hard, while the shadows are deep. This might be the lighting used on a Western, or something on the desert or at sea, very natural looking. Highlights tend to be very hot causing whites and light colors to "Burn Out." Pastels look weak, medium and dark colors work the best. This kind of lighting can also burn out aging and have the effect of "cleaning" the clothes on screen.

High Key/Low Contrast: this would be a bright light, overall, with a lot of fill light to take out the shadows... a musical, comedy or sit-com. Because of the perfect artificial lighting balance, colors of a larger spectrum can be used – there won't be any hot highlights or color lost in shadow. The effect is almost like "abstract painting" with pure colors.

Low Key/High Contrast: Overall, dim (can have very bright spot lighting) but with lots of shadows – a moody piece, film noire, horror. If an overall darkness is required – medium to dark clothing in the cool tones. Whites will look strong and should be dyed down. Jewel tones will look rich. Whites, if used, will look sharp; blacks are great anchor. Self or subtle prints are good to break up color masses.

Low Key/Low Contrast, Overall dim, soft and even, without the dark shadows or blinding highlights; a love story on the Irish coast in the fog. Everything looks good here.

Strobing: Something you have to be conscious of. The picture you see on a television or shot with a video camera is made up of electronic signals called pixels. These signals are like a honeycomb of squares, each square getting information from the electronic "eye" – what color to make itself. If you use a tight pattern, like black and white check, the honeycomb squares can't read the moving print fast enough to change, they get confused and start switching back and forth between the black and white – strobing.

★**Here's something to think about:** Have you ever looked at a crowd of people and seen someone who seemed so out of place that you said to yourself "If I dressed someone that way, I'd be fired"...? Well, I have. The thing is, life isn't perfect and while we are all used to seeing the imperfections that compose reality, we don't really notice them. But, the more "perfect" a thing is, the more false or "unnatural" it strikes us. A musical, the furthest removed from reality, looks the most false or perfect, while a war film or Western, posing as "real drama," is full of facial hair and character wardrobe.

Okay, you kind of know the clothing you want and think you know the best colors – What now? Now's the time to start testing your ideas on paper.

Arab man
Study for type, *The WInd and the Lion*

chapter 12

SKETCHING

SKETCHING:

There are Designers who use Costume Illustrators – great, but what if you don't have access to one? You still have to face showing your design concepts to a host of people, from director to workroom, so it's a skill that you need to cultivate.

While I like to draw and even paint as a hobby, costume sketches scared the heck out of me. Why? Well, I always had a hard time figuring out *whom* the sketch was for and what it was supposed to look like.

★Story: my first film as Costume Designer took me to Spain where I set up shop at a Spanish costume house. I wanted to do well, to create something really wonderful. I agonized over dresses for the leading lady. I poured over period photos, drawings, paintings. I went back to my hotel room every night to draw and redraw her dress. It never looked right, either the dress was wrong or the drawing was stiff. Finally I got it, both the drawing and the dress were "right," at least it was as good as I was going to do. I rushed to show it to the production designer and the director. They loved it. I felt great. I went back to the Spanish costume house workroom. The head cutter-fitter was a middle-aged Spanish woman, thin, droopy eyelashes, a cigarette always at the corner of her mouth. I put my sketch on her cutting table. "This," I announced, "is the dress you'll be making for Miss so-and-so...." She eyed the sketch a moment, took a long puff and answered, "Beautiful darling, how's the back cut?" I looked at my sketch, the one I had poured so many hours into – and I hadn't the faintest idea about the back. I felt really dumb.

You see what I mean? But if you make the sketch too workroom-oriented, showing every seam and panel, it might look too stiff. If it's for the director, then maybe it should be more conceptual — major lines and color. If it's for the actors... should it look like them? Should it be one of those impossibly long-legged sketches from fashion magazines that have a lot of style but tend to look affected and unreal? How does one pick a rendering style that satisfies everyone?

Well, how about more than one sketch?

First, a "Concept" drawing for the director, producer, production designer, showing how you *feel* about the clothes in general: loose, tight, baggy, flowing, the color, the texture, all draped onto a reasonably realistic, human body shape, in loose color on board. The second, a line drawing, intended for the workroom, explaining your ideas in more detail, more blueprint than art, to be attached for your workroom meetings. And last, maybe a "Finished" sketch. Remember, it might be a good idea to do a concept sketch first, swatch the material, *then* do the finished sketch. A finished drawing is just that, a *finished* drawing. Besides, it's not a good idea to sell a concept with a beautiful idea on paper, then have to try and find if the right material exists.

About drawing. I believe that *anyone*, with a desire to draw, can get good, with practice. As far as the human figure goes, there are lots of resources to copy from, and copy you should, over and over, from photos or life, until you "catch the line" that we all recognize as "Human." It gets easier with time.

A little drawing tip: Many people try to draw the way they write, bent over a table top with the pencil cramped in hand, with head down, drawing from the wrist. This might be okay for putting detail in your drawing, however... it's not a good way to start. Start by standing up where you can have the most distant view of your drawing surface and your research. Hold the pencil loosely, keeping the wrist straight and draw using your shoulder. This should give you the ability to capture bigger, sweeping lines, while keeping the drawing in proportion. If you can, use a portable, slanted drawing board or drawing table. Working on a flat surface may distort your vision and your drawing will "angle" across the paper.

If you start a period show, you may want to sit down with a ream of 8½ x 11 paper and some research books. Start copying every costume illustration you think fits what you are doing. Soon, you will develop a good feeling for what lines are repeated over and over. What makes the period, the period. You might also search out and make pencil drawings of costume details — interesting trim, jewelry, anything you think you might incorporate into a drawing later.

Doing this before you sit down to sketch for cast costumes gives you the familiarity with the period that will put confidence in your sketches and give you a knowledge and feeling for things like detail and trim, which will help you design more realistic clothing.

Color? If you're uncertain or insecure with paint, I would start with color pencils, a little at a time. Get going in the right direction. When the drawing starts to look more firm, start adding color with paint in broad areas. I favor acrylics and have never developed any confidence with water color, but I've seen and admired others who could render beautiful costume sketches with watercolor or gouache, and made it look easy.

Any technique or combination of mediums that express your idea to others is fair. There are no rules or "rights and wrongs," except that your rendering is readable, expressive, and helps you sell your ideas; and, remember, they will go into your portfolio.

I have included some sketches of my own. My drawing style has changed over the years, from show to show. Some of the work was done in the safety of my studio at home, some on hastily built drawing boards on location, with the workroom waiting, some are concept sketches or "quick" sketches, some are more complete, but I include them to show the variety of possibilities.

And don't forget, there are many great Costume Illustrators registered with the Costume Designers Guild who help Designers who are too busy or don't feel that they want do the renderings themselves.

I think that the reason some Designers don't want to draw is they feel that they can't. This usually means that they can't draw a human or can't think of how the drawing should stand or what it should be doing (where do you put the hands?) If this is you, this is really a shame, because worrying about your figure drawing is stopping you from seeing your designs come alive on paper and having fun creating them.

There are a few easy ways to create renderings. One way is to repeat the figure — this is called "croquet" — it's easy and it takes your mind off of trying to draw.

1). Start with 8½" x 11" copy paper. Lightly draw a center line vertically down the paper and "head" and "toe" stop lines, horizontally, about an inch from the top and bottom of the paper. Divide the center line into six spaces for a man and seven spaces for a woman.

Now, either freehand a figure or use any photo reference you like and copy or trace the outline of a figure, centered on your center line. Some magazines are full of photos of models standing around in poses you can use and there is also a book titled *New Fashion Figure Templates*, by P. Ireland, with sketched figures you can trace or copy.

If you can't see through the copy paper and don't have a light table, hold the photograph and copy paper against a window and let the sun do the work, while you trace the figure outline.

Erase any hard lines, but leave an image that you can still see. Photocopy the image as many times as you like. Now you don't have to worry about how well you can draw, sketch after sketch. You just draw the clothes you want on the lightly photocopied figure guide.

You can make the sketches more artistic by using colored paper to photocopy onto. I like a medium gray or tan.

You then can copy your costume idea several times and try various color schemes. You'll be surprised how quickly a sketch can come to life with just a little highlight, shadow, and accent coloring. If you don't like an idea, throw it away and reach for another figure guide.

Experiment with colored pencil, colored markers (they bleed) and art pens or charcoal or grease pencils to sharpen and thicken lines.

Finished successful sketches can be put into a 3-ring binder in clear plastic document holders or mounted on foam core or poster board. If mounted on stiff board with spray mount, they can stand some water color and/or acrylic touch-up. (They might wrinkle if glue isn't applied to both sides and the rendering allowed to dry thoroughly.)

2). Once successful with this process, you can go to 8½" x 14" for bigger, bolder drawings.

Christopher Plummer
The New World

Colin Farrell
The New World

J.TURNER

103

1860's
PRAIRIE DRESS

Janine Turner
Stolen Women, Captured Hearts

Pierce Brosnan
The *Broken Chain*

MAN CALLED HORSE II

linen shirt

Richard Harris
The Return of a Man Called Horse

106

Tied shawl
'ld Blanket

weave coat
out of pcs of
Torn cloth

Moccasins
w/wraps

VIRUS - Olivia Hussey

Olivia Hussey
Virus

RAMBO III - Stallone

Jade Buddah on chain

military shoulder Bag for Bombs.

RAMO VIET BOOTS @ $1,500. 6 pair

Sylvester Stallone
Rambo III

Gods & Generals

Robert Duvall
Lee

Robert Duvall as General Robert E. Lee
Gods and Generals

3). Computer-literate people can scan these renderings and manipulate them in PhotoShop, placing them in actual locations or against fanciful backgrounds.

4). You also can trace figure guides on drafting vellum, which is better at taking ink markers. Try the markers on the back of the drawing for a softer overall look, then use colored pencils on the front for details — experiment — have fun!

Of course, if you have some confidence in your drawing ability but need a little direction I like the book, *Essential Fashion Illustration*, a Rockport publication, edited by Maite Lafuente. It has lots of illustrations to look at, in various styles.

CONCLUSION:

You now should have a pretty good budget package that you can explain, with research that backs up your direction, and some sketches of cast members' costumes with swatches that illustrate your design direction. By this time, you also will be very conversant about the upcoming shoot with an eye on anticipating potential problems.

Once you've successfully concluded all your concept and budget meetings and have gotten a production "Go Ahead," you can get to work. I know how funny that sounds, after getting this far and doing this much, but everything up until now has been getting ready for work; you've built your show on paper. Now, the real work of building a physical show begins. The production clock is ticking.

One page of storyboard for *Pearl Harbor* attack

chapter **13**

PRODUCTION MEETINGS

Sometime before shooting, everyone gets together in a meeting presided over by a member of production and goes through the script, page by page, for red flags or production information. Most of the time, specific wardrobe questions are left for another, private meeting with the Director... but, what about the rest of the crew?

On any film project there are several departments represented. All of you have to work together... so who does what and how can you prepare for them?

Politics aside, departments interact, professionally, according to their departments' interests and objectives. If you can understand those, then you can better understand what will be required of your department, by whom and when. Being able to anticipate those relationships will allow you to prepare for them and not be caught off guard when sudden demands come at you "out of nowhere." The good news is, for every shoot you will ever be on, the jobs will stay the same; your only "wild-card" will be negotiating through the various personalities who hold these positions, show by show.

Remember: Everyone on your show has seen someone else do your job, perhaps many times — they know what they feel can be expected.

On standard budget forms, "creative talent," Producers, Directors, writers, and actors are separated from "labor" by a line (for sub-totaling expenditures). Everyone listed as creative talent is "Above the Line," everyone listed as labor is "Below the Line." You are "Below the Line," along with the other departments. Because of their functions, "Above the Line"

111

personnel are management or "talent," and they have the ultimate power on a shoot, while other "Below the Line" departments are more or less your equal, in terms of cooperation.

Because of this, we'll go down the list, as to whom you will meet, what they (most likely) will want and how they can affect you and your job.

*When movie production first began, the pioneers looked for a business model to follow. They picked the construction industry. So, the script is like a "blueprint," the Producers are the "Developers," the Unit Production Manager (U.P.M.) is the "General Contractor," the First Assistant Director (First AD) is the "Job Foreman," and the departments are the "trades." They still call the filmmaking process: "Developing a Property."

THE PRODUCER:

The Producer is the first person on. It is **his** or **her** project... but there are different levels of Producer-hood.

THE EXECUTIVE PRODUCER:

You may never meet this person. The Executive Producer gets the money to fund. Sometimes the Executive Producer will never show up, the job being more a function of money than the day-to-day process of shooting the film. My experience is that they leave the creative decisions up to others — not to say that getting the funding together isn't creative.

The Producer will be the immediate head of production.

It may be that this person had the idea, originally, took it to the Executive Producer for funding, and is now entrusted with delivering the film for exhibition, for the dollar amount raised. It may be that this person owns a production company and is delivering this project to the Executive Producer for exhibition, for a pre-agreed budget. There may be more than one Producer representing various production entities; either way, the Producer is the boss. Sometimes the Producer has very definite ideas about the "look" of the project, sometimes not. Sometimes interest is more dramatic or financial. Either way, you work for the Producer.

The Producer will always want, and be entitled to have, something to say about the look of the production. Many times, that vision can't be articulated, except in the general sense of wanting it to be "good" or "realistic"; sometimes Producers are very sophisticated about technical matters, including sets, costumes, and props.

A concept meeting, early on, with the Producers, is important. Find out where their heads are. They always will have the interest — the question is "How demanding do they want to be?" They may leave you alone, or they may be people you have to try and convince. They may demand that you do something you hate; and they may know more about it than you do — you have to find out. Be relaxed and courteous, it's their show and you're there to help them.

THE LINE PRODUCER:

Also found under Unit Production Manager. The Line Producer has the direct responsibility of making the film, day-to-day, within pre-determined budget guidelines. He or she hires the workforce. Many technicians aim their responsibility at this position. This person works show-to-show and often re-hires the same people — people who are financially responsible and, at the same time, please the Producer and Director with their results. Usually not dictatorial about the "look," the Line Producer is always budget and schedule centered, hating to spend money not in the budget — but very interested in your budget and your ideas on running your department. This is the person to whom you will have to justify your numbers. These folks are usually industry savvy, have a lot of budget experience and have hired and seen your job done before by someone else. A sound, well-prepared department plan will go a long way with this person. When convinced of your position, this person will be the one to get you what you need. They **never like surprises**! Talk to them, weekly, on expenditures and projections. Tell them *immediately* if you think you're going over the budget discussed.

★I once worked for an English Production Manager who never said much. When I thanked him for his non-interference he replied, "Well old boy, if you hire a professional crew, then tell them what to do, it's like buying a dog and barking, yourself." Love those English.

THE DIRECTOR:

Most people know what this job is. Originally a job more technical than creative, the Director was charged with getting performances out of the

113

actors, while the staging was left to the Cinematographer. The Director worked more with the Editor in shooting the required angles to splice together to form the storytelling montages, while the design was left to the Art Director (sets) and Costume Designer (including Hair and Make-up). All this has changed with the "Author" concept of filmmaking, Now, the Director is the **final authority** on the set and for what goes before the camera. Well, almost.

The Director is the person who will feel in direct control. The Director has been hired by the Producer to use his or her moviemaking skill and *taste*, to get what needs to be gotten on film. Everything needs the Director's stamp of approval. For this reason, **concept** meetings with the Director are a must! The Director will be keenly interested in the Costume Illustration. The Director's job is to dovetail all the elements: Photography, Lighting, Sets, Costumes, Effects, Editing, and actors' performances into a credible, visual, dramatic interpretation. In a sense, they are also the "Directors of Design," and you have to work closely with them to come to a shared vision that you can pour yourself into: research; "Show-and-Tells"; "Costume Parades"; concept sketches... whatever it takes.

A word about the Director's authority. Directors have all the authority that the Producers agree to let them have, according to their deals and the budgets.

There can be a problem here that you will meet on production, and it's called, "Who's show is it, anyway?" These are times when the Line Producer and the Director are not sharing the same vision.

Example: The Director tells you to get overcoats for everybody. You hire the overcoats... telling the Line Producer, who says, "Tell the Director, No! They're not in the budget," What do you do? I would advise this: If anybody, Director and Producer included, ask you for anything in addition to your agreed budget, be calm, positive, and optimistic, get a dollar amount and talk to the Line Producer. On some shows, the money is there, the Director may be the Producer and the answer will be, "What are you waiting for?" but this won't always be the answer. Sometimes the answer will be a very definite "NO!" Find out before you spend money. If there is a production department disagreement about what should or shouldn't be spent, get them to talk to each other.

THE FIRST ASSISTANT DIRECTOR:

Known as the "First AD." If the Directors direct the cast, then the "Firsts" direct the crew. The set belongs to them. They are directly responsible to the Line Producer to get the crew organized and keep the Director on schedule. Their problems are many. They do not like surprises or excuses. They run the "AD Department," which is, officially, the "Eyes and Ears of Production." They belong to the same Director's Guild as the Director and Unit Manager or Line Producer... and they talk together about everything and everyone on the show.

They also have a hand in scheduling and coming up with the "Extra day count." You want to jump on the First Assistant Directors, as soon as they're hired, to get a fix on how many extras you will enjoy on any one set and their latest thoughts on the schedule; both of these pieces of information are **crucial** to your department. How many costumes do you need, what works first and where? The impact on your work schedule is dynamic. Everything you do, department-wise, apart from the creative, will be to facilitate **their** set operation and schedule. Get them **used** to your asking questions. Be persistent in getting show-schedule information, then match your department needs against it. Build a relationship that will be lasting and cooperative. This will be your biggest source of "inside information."

115

THE SECOND ASSISTANT DIRECTOR:

This is the person who implements work on the set, while the First is busy around camera. The Second will be the person you find around the dressing rooms and setting background action. If the First is unreachable, the Second is your best bet for production information, including call sheets and advance schedules. They also help wrangle extras and do most of the production paperwork.

THE PRODUCTION DESIGNER:

This title never used to exist. They used to be called "Art Directors" and their jobs were to design and oversee the construction of the sets and their decoration. Sometime in the '70s, they created the job of "Production Designer," because it was felt that one person had to sit with the Director from Day One to "Concept" the show. Everything that went in front of the camera was part of a cohesive design concept that fell under the purview of the "Production Designer."

This is a relationship that you will have to feel out. Most Production Designers are not costume-trained and don't want to take over your department... but in the initial phases will want to, and have the right to, comment on the direction of your design concept. They are **big** on color. Everything you know about color theory, color percentage and value, will be a help. They tend to put a lot of stock into old paintings, as research. With regard to color usage, see Rembrandt, Norman Rockwell, Frederick Remington, Winslow Homer, N. C. Wyeth, and John Singer Sergeant, for openers.

Professional courtesy is the key. Remember, they were usually on the show first and have had more discussions with the Director about the "look" than you have. These are, generally, seasoned professional artists, usually with backgrounds in architecture. Once they find that what you're doing is cool, they'll let you do your thing... listen, learn, be happy.

THE TECHNICAL ADVISOR:
Some are a bigger influence than others with the Director. I always make it a point to talk to them as early as I can and go over everything with them. If they have a problem with anything that affects my budget, I get a meeting with the Line Producer and find out what the company wants me to do. Do I rent the uniform that isn't quite right, but close, or do I spend more to build the "correct" one that the T. A. wants? (read more at the end of the chapter on Costume Design, by Capt. Dale Dye.)

THE SCRIPT SUPERVISOR:
They take notes on everything that is photographed to help the Director get the shots needed for the editorial process, later. You want to check your wardrobe plot, especially your "story days," with this person. Most Supervisors will tell you that they expect "wardrobe" to attend to its own matching because they are watching everything else — which is true.

THE CAMERA DEPARTMENT:
They call this business, "**Motion Pictures**," not "Motion Sound" or "Motion Costumes." The Director of Photography, or "DP" is the head recordist. This is another relationship that you have to feel out... but generally, the DP is there to photograph it, not dictate what it looks like. The mutual area of concern will be color, especially whites and off-whites. If,

on a shooting day, they say that they can't photograph a costume because it's too bright — everything stops while you fix it. Very ugly — have a talk with the DP about color during the early stages of preparation.

MAKE-UP/HAIR DRESSING DEPARTMENT:

As a Designer, the biggest interface will concern facial hair, hair styles, and the wearing of hats or hair ornaments. This includes anything Native Americans (or anyone else) might wear in their hair, or material for braid-ties. Women's hats are set in and pinned in the hair trailer, as well, meaning that they have to be taken there and collected every day. Hair style research, especially for cast, should be shared between Designer, Hair Person and Director to agree on the "look." Things tend to get lost in doing crowds, braid wraps, feathers, custom-made ornaments. Get more than you think you need.

THE PROPERTY DEPARTMENT:

My favorite. If Costumers are "Rag Pickers" then Prop people are "Junkers." The best "on set" working relationship you can have will be with the Prop Person. All the "stuff" on the set, everything the Decorator left behind to dress, belongs to the Prop Person. Everything your actor removes or puts on, during the course of a scene, belongs to the Prop Person. All jewelry, watches, bags, swords, guns, props. If you read, in the script, that a particular piece of wardrobe has "Action"... it's an "Action Prop," and belongs to the Prop Person.

"Wardrobe" and "Property" have to help each other build the show together.

On shows like Westerns or action movies, where a lot of belt equipment, helmets, and the like is worn, the question always arises, "Who will carry this or that and whose budget will it come out of?" The old rule of thumb was, if it goes in a dressing room for actors and they go to make-up with it, it's Costume. If it's issued off a truck **after** the actor/extra is dressed, it's a Prop. If it's handed to the actor and taken from the actor on the set... it's a prop. If it has described action... it's a prop.

No matter what, there **will** be crossover pieces between Costumes and Property... work it out early. The Property Department can be your biggest asset on the set, if you have a good working relationship. These can be clever, artistic, and very knowledgeable people. Work together — they are interested in the same things you are, as far as actor character is concerned, just different stuff.

Before production starts you may have a 'Show-and-Tell' with Production — always invite the Property Master. It's good to show costumes completed with jewelry, watches, and other accessories that the Property Master will be responsible for.

THE DECORATOR:

Heads the "Set-Dec" department and is responsible for everything that furnishes the set. They will ask you for clothes to dress the sets. Suitcases, drawers, clotheslines. My answer is always, "I can only afford enough clothes to dress the people I have to. If you need clothes for dressing, please give me a list and I'll rent them for you on your department budget, or you can select them yourself. After the show, **you** will be responsible to return them to the rental house, thank you." There are times when they want to use a piece of principal wardrobe because it will tie a character in... and that's okay, I'll give it to them before the shot and take it back after the shot... but in general, costumes are costumes and dressing is dressing. If they lose or destroy something they borrow, you will pay for it, plus, you will lose the use of the clothes while they have them, maybe longer than you think. Have them get their own. The production meeting is a good place to ask them if they need anything.

THE STUNT DEPARTMENT:

Another one of my favorites. I've had a lot of friends in this department over the years and, as a set person, was detailed, many times, to take care of them and their costume needs. They are, by definition, hard on clothes.

I always make it a point to get hold of the Stunt Coordinator as soon as I can and find out the sizes of the stunt crew, who will be doubling the cast (with sizes), and what, if any, safety rigging or equipment will be necessary, including fireproofing or flying-rig harnesses. If it's an action piece, will the clothes (which look tight on the actor), have to be gusseted for the stunt double who has to perform the action? Will the leather-sole shoes have to be covered with rubber for non-slip traction? If I don't get answers on sizes, I take oversized clothes for them to wear over stunt pads.

The **Stunt Coordinator** might also be the **Second Unit Director**. Now's the time to find out how ambitious that second unit will be and whether or not you'll need both extra clothes and help to service them.

★On Westerns or war films, the amount of multiples used for bullet hits, progressive aging, and hard-use destruction can be hard on your department budget, if you're not prepared for it.

THE TRANSPORTATION DEPARTMENT:

"Transpo," rolling stock, and sometimes tents on location are "Transpo" items. They will know where to rent wardrobe trucks and trailers. I've always found that these people do what they can to help facilitate your needs. Give them as much advance warning as possible about the movement and location spotting of your equipment. These guys work hard and keep the company rolling — help them. They may also drive the "picture cars" in the shot and require costumes. Find out from the Transportation Captain who, if anyone, will appear on camera and get their sizes early.

THE ACCOUNTING DEPARTMENT:

Their functions are "time card/payroll" and purchase orders (POs), petty cash, and vendor payments. Timecard/payroll speaks for itself. Whatever PO system your company is on is usually cumbersome and not geared for speed of purchase.

Some of your immediate purchase problems can be solved with a "Petty Cash" draw. I always walk my vendor bills through Accounting to be sure that they are paid promptly. I tend to use a lot of the same vendors over and over. I have business-friendly relationships with them. If I need something right away, I know that I can call several sources and they will send me the things I need, immediately, **on my word**. They do this because they know that I will take care of their bills as soon as they come in, period. Your ability to pull rabbits out of hats is only as good as your sources.

I also get used to checking with the show accountant on the status of my department expenditures on a weekly basis, to keep track of where I am, in relation to my budget.

119

THE CASTING DEPARTMENT:

Here's where the actors come from... information you want ASAP. Let them get used to your phone calls, so when they sign someone, they're reminded to call you right away. On location they will have a "Local" casting person who gets local crowds together. This is the person you need to talk to, to get people in for fittings. You can also discuss the sizes of clothing you have and ask that they fill those sizes — they can try.

THE EFFECTS DEPARTMENT:

Again, by definition, hard on clothes. Find out early what their requirements are for multiples of costumes. If there will be large battle scenes, you might want to park your department close to the effects truck — those will be days when you'll have to work together.

WRANGLERS:

Mostly on Westerns. They will always drive the wagons and sometimes ride horses in the shot. They are the hardest people to keep track of because they work both before and after shooting with the livestock. I love them but, they get used to throwing the clothes in the back of the horse trailer, then bringing them back in a dirty pile.

THE PRODUCTION COORDINATOR:

This person can save your life on location. A good Production Coordinator will get shipments in and out for you, when you need something and are locked on the set. They know when the actors arrive and where they are staying. They can and will try and set up fittings for you, including getting the actor transported to the set and back.

THE GRIP DEPARTMENT:

These people handle the set carpentry, camera movement, and lighting diffusion. I always start a show by telling the Key Grip that I have access to a sewing machine and will be happy to make sandbags, repair their silks, add "floppies" to their flags, etc. When working the set I always helped them move apple boxes or whatever. Grips carry century, or "C" stands to hold their diffusion. These "C" stands can be used for temporary clothes racks on location, behind camera. They are usually happy to let you use them; be sure to return them when you're finished or next time they "might not have enough."

THE ELECTRIC DEPARTMENT:

These folks might hook up your work lights, lend you extension cords, or help your department with some electrical problem; be kind.

THE SOUND DEPARTMENT:

This is a department that will work with the Set Costumer all the time in the placing of microphones, wires, transmitters. I check with the Sound Technicians to see if they need small pouches with waist ties to secure their transmitters around the waists of the actors, and if they don't have them, I make them.

If Sound doesn't have these pouches, they may cut holes inside your pants or coat pockets to string the wire from the microphone to the transmitter in the actors' pockets.

Every expendables store carries "Sound Booties." These are black or white, slip-on overshoes made of flannel; they're designed to muffle foot-falls on wood floors.

The Sound Department hates silk. Sensitive sound equipment hears the "rustle" of a silk tie or blouse when the microphone is a small clip-on type.

There are other jobs on a shoot: Greens, Locations, Catering, Craft Service, Teachers, Medics and more, but your professional contact with them will be limited, as far as Costumes go.

121

Example for Cover

chapter 14

ACCUMULATING COSTUMES

First, you have to develop an angle of attack. What I mean by this is that you have to have a plan; and that plan has to be specific to your show and department requirements. How and where are you going to get the things that you need?

Part of the problem has been solved by a couple of things that you've already done. Your Costume Breakdown and Budget Package have, in them, the amounts and types of costumes, researched, that you'll be looking for and a schedule telling you when and where your costumes will start working.

You have two main requirements: cast and background. The Designer usually starts addressing the cast requirements (stock, shopping, manufacture?), while the Supervisor organizes the labor to assemble the background clothing according to the agreed-upon "look" — the Designer always checks the pulling progress for "look" conformity. The Designer also has to face pulling actor-fitting time out of the accumulation schedule, before shipping and shooting.

On "modern" projects, where you can find most of what you need by shopping, you may have to hire costumers as "shoppers" — the accumulation of stock for fittings might include lots of "taking things out on approval" and returning the unused items later. Stores hate this. Don't be tempted to use anything and try to return it later, as unused, by replacing the tags. I used to purchase everything for fittings and use the clothing, unused on cast, for background later.

SMALL PROJECTS: (basically under a hundred outfits.)
Many people are involved with commercials, print ad, or small film projects in a regional area that isn't convenient to major costume rental houses. If this is your situation, then you know to depend more on yourself and a network of vendors and local craftspeople to fill your needs; these sources might include local theater or college drama departments. If you get a requirement for things that exceed your local resources and if you're not convenient to major costume rental houses, they're easy to find (some listed in the back). Call them, ask if they have the stock you need. If they sound helpful and knowledgeable, talk overall concept, as well as specifics. They might have some good ideas, based on the stock they know they have. Expect to pay $50, or so, to have them send you digital photos, online, of examples of the stock you're looking for. Be prepared to fax them simple line drawings of what you want (photos and/or photocopies don't fax well), or mail more complete packages. Discuss prices — both short-term, weekly, and long-term production, and rental prices, as they will differ from house to house.

124

    If it's a phone order to a costume house, have all your business information ready — name, business name, fax and phone number, billing address, shipping address, credit card number, with name and address of card holder, FedEx account number, date you need the costumes, date you will ship the costumes back, a concise list of the costumes you need, their colors, and their sizes.

    ★Speaking of sizes, women's dress sizes are usually not good to go by; women's dress sizes change with period, pattern, maker and label — a size eight from the '40s might fit a size four today. Always get a bust, waist, hip, height, neck, sleeve, and depending on the length of the garment, a waist-to-knee and waist-to-floor, and/or a waist-to-hem measurement. Men's clothes are usually sized that way anyway, but with men, always give the pant-inseam length, since the out-seam length will vary from period to period, with the cut (high-rise, low-rise). Remember, with '30s and '40s pants, the rise is so high that men can wear a shorter inseam because of the drop in the crotch.

    If you have a little lead time, ask the costume house if you can establish credit. It's easy to get the costume house accountant to send you a credit application, which you can have the company you're working for fill out and return. This way, you can order and the company will be billed with no charges to the credit card (which you might want to save for other things). If you have to use a credit card, expect a "reserve" hold on the card against Loss and Damage equal to two to three times the rental.

RENTAL HOUSES AND THE PACKAGE DEAL:

Larger projects (where you will get the clothes and the kind of money deal favorable to you), will take some analyzing; so it might be good to look at the internal workings of a costume house first.

A costume house is, first and foremost, a business. In order to stay in business, it has to meet its obligated expenses. It has to make money by renting, selling, or making costumes to fill show requirements for Designers and Supervisors, and ultimately for producers and studios.

There are two ways to look at any business relationship: Partnership or Adversarial.

Sometimes people hired on a show will put themselves in an adversarial position with the very people they need to help them.

Let's look at where you are and what you're trying to do at this point: You are hired and have a commitment to deliver a show's requirements. You have an amount of money to work with (never enough), and a finite amount of time to round up all your requirements and be somewhere else to start shooting.

Your objectives are threefold: 1) Get everything you can; 2) as fast as you can; 3) as cheaply as you can.

What's the costume house's business mission? 1) Give you what they can; 2) as fast as they can; 3) for as much as they can.

Some people favor competitive shopping; it goes like this... "How much do you charge for a shirt?... How much do you charge for a dress?" You do this with your list of requirements, times the amount of costume houses you can find. You learn that all the prices are about the same; you might hear that this one will give you a discount or that one will beat "anyone's price." You then try and figure out where you can stretch your rental budget further, since you also are trying to figure out how much you should keep back for manufacture and purchases... it's you against the world.

When you start "pulling" from every house in town, you find that no one has much time to help you. You explain that you are trying to "spread" your money around because you owe a favor or because you want to "help everyone a little." You ask for a discount and are refused because "Your order is too small." You feel disgruntled when you're told that you can't just rent "partial" outfits or that "We don't accessorize."

Think Wal-Mart. How do they charge such low prices? Volume. From a costume house point of view, the more you take, including purchases and manufacture, the more they can lower the price. Why? Easy. Let's say that your budget is $50.000, but you are quoted $50,000 in rentals, plus $10,000 in purchases — you can't afford it. You plead with the costume house to give you $50,000 worth of rentals for $40,000 so you can afford the $10,000 for purchases. They say "no," maybe 10%, that's it. What can you do? You keep shopping around, while your time runs out.

From the costume house side, if I were the manager, I would have to look at the "business" of your show. You want "X" amount of clothing. I have a "price book" with company-set prices. I have to think about how much of *my* labor I will have to spend to get my side of your show ready. I may have to spend a certain amount to complete outfits that you've ordered. I have a price sheet that's fair and competitively priced. I know that you're getting things from other places. In some cases, you're not even getting complete outfits from me. You've found cheaper prices somewhere else, but like some of my stuff better, so you want to get the suits from "Joe" down the block, and want to rent the hats and shoes from me. Well, my answer would be "No." Why? Number one, you aren't being a good customer... sorry, that's the answer. Two, no way am I going to accessorize your show with hats and shoes. Why not? If I let you take my hats and shoes and the next costumers want to rent complete outfits, I won't be able to rent them complete outfits... because you have the hats and shoes. If you've broken everything up into small units based on competitive pricing or individual service prices, I have to stick to my prices, because everything I give you will have to "pay for itself." This will result in more pressure on you and not much savings.

This will be a "no-win situation" for everyone and is adversarial.

What's the answer? Partnership. Same situation: You tell me that you only have $50,000, but you need $50,000 worth of rentals and $10,000 worth of purchases. Instead of sitting across the table, we take chairs on the same side. We find out how we can do this together, based on the amount *you* have to spend. Be frank, open, honest — your financial situation or requirements won't change, but the attitude of the costume house will.

As the manager, I have to assess whether I want your purchases. If I do, then I might make that deal, give you everything, rentals and purchases, for the $50,000 you have to spend. Why? Easy, I'm using the rental profit to absorb your purchases — provided I get them back, where I will be able to count them as equity for my **future** rental profit.

That combining of budget requirements, rentals, purchases, and manufacture into a lump-sum, bottom-line figure is called a "package deal," and it always works the same way — it uses the power of the money spent in rentals to absorb the cost of purchases and/or manufacture. If you only are talking about lowering the price of the rentals, you can still call it a "package," but it's really just a discounted rental price.

The financial ability of any costume house to lower prices by combining elements in your budget will always be based on the rental volume you do with them because, the more business you give them, on "off-the-rack" stock items, the larger rental-income base it gives them to spread other costs over... amortization.

Always look at the hanging stock in a rental house with this in mind. Find the house that has **the most** stock that can go toward your show and construct your package deal there. If you want things from other places, talk about it ahead of time, reserve some of your budget money for "outside rentals." Find out how much they will throw in, if you do the bulk of the show there; office, cage, discount on a trailer? Most places know that they are competing for the same dollars on your show, so when they see that you're serious, they get serious.

You can use your cast and background breakdown sheets to give them an idea of what's required of them. Figure out and tell them how much of your show you can do from their stock and how much you expect them to make or buy. They can figure out if they can afford to work with you within your budget or not.

Another thing that you might want to consider: when you are on a distant location, have an emergency and have to call back to town for help... whom do you want on the other end of the line? Who has the best reserve of stuff, and who is the most dependable and/or has a bigger financial interest in you and your show?

If you plan to have anything made at a costume house with costume house labor, discuss everything in advance. Sometimes people are not clear on who owns what at the end of the show, or are put off by a 25% or 35% addition to a manufacture price for Loss and Damage, especially after they paid to have it made. The house answer is: "We made it for you at our cost. If you don't return it, we have to add on our profit margin or we did it for nothing." That always confused me until I really thought about it.

Sometimes, the deal will be easy; just a straight forward rental. No matter what the size or shape of the deal is, you will need to arrange to pay them something, sometime.

Of course, when striking any deal, be sure to address the Loss and Damage prices. Find out, in advance, what the house plans to charge you, in both general and specific prices. If they give you a good deal going in, then you might expect "full-book" replacement on the way out. See if they will accept exchanges for losses — your location purchases or outside manufacture items, for example. On the bottom of most rental contracts is a line that says that they will charge up to 10 times the rental price for a loss or damage, with an outfit rental cost of $250 to $350 — that could be a lot of money.

You also will have to determine a "bench-mark, draw-down schedule," which means the dates your company is required to pay the house. Sometimes, it's a third down, another third half way through prep, and the last third before the costumes leave the house. Sometimes, it's half down and half before the costumes leave. Sometimes, you will have until the end of the show to finish paying, and sometimes it can be something else, but you have to work this out, along with the size of the deposit for Loss and Damage, and final show cleaning.

On shows where the costume house and the producer are at odds over price or payment schedule, you can find yourself in the middle of **their** negotiation, being asked to carry figures back and forth. If this happens, I would advise to get **them** together to work things out and stand back until **they** are both satisfied that the deal **they** agree to, is the best deal **they** can make. Being in the middle puts you in an awkward position with everyone — but show politics may dictate that you get in there and try your hand at negotiating.

The company, your employer, will of course, expect that you get the best price you can for them. If you are dedicated to your budget, you will want to get the best deal you can for your department. In this sense, you are acting as an "agent" for your employer; you have the legal, fiduciary duty to act in their best interest.

However, as a professional Costume Designer, you also will have an understanding for the problems of the rental house. You will, in a professional sense, understand that the costume house has to make some money in order to stay in business and continue to be a resource for you in the future.

Somewhere within those interests lies the deal that everyone can live with. It takes a special attitude to negotiate successfully; you have to understand everyone's interests but give your department requirements' first priority... see where one side or the other can give and point it out to them, while keeping in good spirits. You want a deal that everyone thinks of as "fair" (while hoping that it's a little more fair to you.)

When you realize that a costume budget can run into the thousands, and hundreds of thousands of dollars, you can easily imagine that you are sitting at the table in a high-stakes card game, and in fact, that's how a lot of people look at it. Raises, bluffs, and all. There are several good books out on negotiating.

One last thing: always go into a meeting with a pad and pencil and write down every deal point that you make — every projected cost, including space and office rental, cost to refurbish rental stock, extended rental costs, manufacture and Loss and Damage charges, packing and shipping charges, "who gets what" at the end, plus delivery schedule (then date the notes and publish them back to the costume house and your production manager) because, later, someone might forget and an "I thought you said" may be countered with, "I don't remember that." Those are bad conversations. And, like every other business, they have "attitude pricing." Be nice — you're building relationships. Remember the old saying: "You might cross the desert with a hundred different caravans, but you will always drink at the same few wells."

Okay, you've made your deal, now it's time to get the clothes.

PULLING YOUR SHOW:

They used to tell us at Fox, "Look at everything two ways, what it is and what it can be." If you can't find what you want, what's close to it?

The object is to get everything you can use, as fast as you can. The reasons are these: 1) You want to see what you have to work with, so that you can find any problem areas that are unexpected and have the most time to address them; 2) You want to look for anything that might be "cast" material, for wear, or samples; and 3) You want to get everything you can, that you like, before someone else, pulling a similar show, gets it. As they used to tell me — get your list and make your count!

Your background breakdown pages are your guide. You can break them up between your labor force and have everyone (or you alone) look for and complete a costume pull, one page at a time, one group at a time. The way things are hung in most costume houses is by like groups. If you're pulling a page of "police," most of it will be together. You can complete each group, check the color and sizes, check for completeness (additional costume house purchases required to fill holes?), repairs, etc. Get that group checked off, start the billing out process and move to the next group.

Just a couple of things to keep in mind while pulling:

Always check the garment for needed repairs. Always check the inside waistband of men's pants for alterations; if they have been taken in a lot, then the leg will be too wide proportionally. Check pant cuffs and dress hems for "let down." If they don't have any, be sure that they make your minimum-length requirement.

I always try and pull my groups of outfits by size, going from small to large, and make sure that if I'm taking five small hats, then I'm also taking five small shirts, coats, vests, pants, and shoes. You don't want to start issuing clothes to extras and discover that you pulled everything you liked because of the color and texture, and now, you are half way through your fittings and have only "small" coats, "large" vests and "medium" pants left, and can't make an outfit that fits anyone. Also, I put up sizes on a curve, 5% to 10% small, 15% to 20% medium, 50% to 60% large, with 10% of those "Longs," 10% to 15% extra large and 5% double extra large. These outfits may have to be broken apart and grouped by type for bulk billing.

Check first.

★Tip: always take a cross section of clothing in black, as well as a few really large sizes — these can come in handy when nothing else works. Always look for good character and gag pieces on every pull from stock.

130

Try to find those special items that will give the leading cast members some "honest" wardrobe to salt their outfits with, and anticipate the day when you will get to fit the extra crowds and featured bit parts, knowing that you'll be able to make interesting and unusual characters whenever you want to.

Check with casting about the area of your location and the average size of the people there and/or if production has given casting any direction about the general look of the extras they want.

Remember that it takes time for the costume house to write up and bill out your order — if you are against a tight time schedule, check with them first and pull your order, or order it for delivery accordingly.

PURCHASES:

If you're looking for unusual things, things not sold in stores at the mall... look online and at the magazine stand first. There are a lot of areas of "special interest," that have a large enough following to have their own "interest" magazines. Everything from sports to "militaria" to antiques have their own devoted magazines and, usually, the backs of those magazines are full of special-interest ads — from vendors who specialize in making and selling things to people who share that interest. That and a diligent phone pursuit, based on business-to-business directories, will usually pay off. And now, of course, we have the world at our finger tips, via the computer.

*Note: This part of preparation always includes lots of petty-cash spending. When you are hired you can draw a "float" from the accountant's office. Have a system ready. It's easy to let money spread out around the department with shoppers rushing this way and that way for things needed now, but, be sure the receipts are accounted for and turned in to you daily for balancing! Receipts should be clear-taped down to copy paper with a date and page total in the bottom corner. If you draw $1,000, turn in $500 (or less) at a time to keep your float revolving; it might take accounting a few days to reimburse you. I always used to keep company money in a separate large wallet with a pocket calculator so it wouldn't get confused with my personal money. Once the receipts are taped and the pages are filled out, they are put into a petty-cash envelope, with all the receipts listed on the front and totaled. Photocopy the face of every envelope for your files before turning the envelope into accounting.

MANUFACTURE:

The reasons to take on any manufacture are simple: Either you can't find what you want hanging for rent or purchase, or you expect a lot of Loss and Damage and don't want to pay twice. Before you embark on a course of manufacture, you have to assess the various means and their advantages/drawbacks.

MAKING CLOTHES:

There are only three ways to do it and they all have different time demands and budget considerations — research prices before making a decision:

1) Have them made at a costume house that is set up for manufacture with its own workroom and/or contractor.

2) Find "outside" sewing contractors or "cut and sew" places, shopping the fabric yourself and doing the contracting.

3) Set up your own workroom.

132

ONE – THE COSTUME HOUSE:

Most costume houses have in-house tailor shops where they do their own alterations and light manufacture. I say "light" manufacture because costume houses aren't set up for mass-production, factory-type work, but individual garment construction. If you want to make suits or dresses for the leading cast, this might be a good option. Prices can vary but because they are all union shops, they pay decent wages and are sometimes more expensive than you would think. This might be offset by the fact that they usually have fabric sources and supplies on the premises, and that the workroom help is as good as you will find anywhere, and better than most places. These are professional costume and clothing makers with years of experience and the costume house will stand behind their work.

They are used to working with both Designers and Stars and are very conscious of deadlines, workmanship, and the fact that what they do will be photographed for the "Big Screen."

The costume houses have access to, and first-hand knowledge of, many workroom people, which takes the guesswork out of hiring for you. Overall, costume house manufacture, or M.O. work ("made-to-order") is very dependable, but it's a good idea to get estimates first.

All the big houses have access to sewing contractors who can deliver large-scale orders.

TWO – FARMING IT OUT:

This usually is thought of when faced with building great numbers of "like" things — armies for example. This entails finding a sewing contractor or a "cut and sew" business that will make room in its production schedule to help you. The burden for design, direction, samples, material is all on you and if their quality control is sloppy, it doesn't matter, you pay for it. You may find problems with lack of seam allowance, grading to larger or smaller sizes, finished work that is measured "seam to seam," rather than with an allowance for fit, and the ever-present "It won't be ready for another week." That being said, the good news is that there are many who are good and will help you if you can afford the time to find them. In the end, it might be better to let a costume house accomplish this scale and type of work for you. They all have done it before, have their own favorite contractors, and understand the steps in making and finishing large manufacture orders. You will, of course, pay for their participation, but that is almost always offset by the dependability factor.

133

If you choose to contract out (even small projects), be sure to have a contract. Be sure of everything; who pays for materials, overtime, who pays for shipping, the date when samples are to be approved, finished delivery date! That **everything**, is spelled out.

Dealing with a vendor for the first time? You will want to "goose" up the final delivery date in order to ensure that if the vendor is a little late, it still won't hurt.

Most vendors will want 50% down and 50% on delivery. Expect that and budget accordingly.

THREE – SETTING UP A WORKROOM:

On shows where you have a shortfall of rentable stock and a large amount of diverse items to come up with, this might make the most sense.

Let's say that you have a Western to do and you realize that you need sets of triple shirts or dresses that you can't find, or have to do a tribe of Indians that doesn't exist on the rack, or are working on a period where the available stock is thin... or due to circumstances, have to make clothes on location.

Outside commercial sewing contractors, while good at mass-production, might not be able to respond to the variety of cutting on small, individual amounts within a large order and would not be able to offer you the fulltime access to oversee the work or its finishing.

Setting up a workroom (discussed somewhat in the budget section), is a very deliberate operation that takes experience and good management. As always, time and money are the enemies. If you're going to try this, hire the best, most experienced Supervisor you can to work out the four-wall facility details.

When it comes to clothing manufacture, it all starts with the cutter/fitter; this is the person whose knowledge, skill, and experience will determine the look and fit of the finished garment. From their hands, the work will pass down through the "Table Lady" to the finishing tailors.

The best cutter/fitters in the world are in the motion picture industry (on the West Coast, they are represented by Costumers Local #705, (323-851-0220). The reason is simple — they are the ones who have worked in every period. Most "outside" cutters have only worked in limited areas: wedding gowns, fashion, ready-to-wear, and while they are good at what they do, usually don't have the experience that "Hollywood" cutters have, with regards to the variety of clothing and end result of being worn on the screen. Also, most "outside" cutters use the **Block** pattern method for arriving at patterns. While "block" pattern cutting is good for modern clothing, it's not the way that period clothes were cut, and rendering a period coat or dress without the correct draping will result in a garment that won't look right.

In resent years, there's been a rush to make things with "re-enactor" clothing people. While these people have a love of history and are sometimes very adamant about the "correctness" of their living-history wear, their quality of manufacture and finishing is sometimes not to industry standards. While a lot of it is passable for background, you might want something more professionally constructed for cast members.

If you are on a union show, your manufacture labor has to be union. Many a Designer has succumbed to the temptation to hire someone they know who is non-union, only to pay a fine later; check with Local #705 for details.

Setting yourself up to run a workroom is challenging but rewarding, also. Be sure to give it a lot of thought and work it out on paper first. Consider: What are we going to build? How much space will it take and how long will I need that space for? Where will that space be and how much will it cost? What kind of shop equipment will be required and where will it come from? What kind of labor will be needed, in terms of experience and expertise and what will that cost be? What will have to be done in order to meet the production schedule?

It's hard work and takes a lot of planning but it's very doable; and you probably won't have to work long as a Designer before you want to, or have to, try it. The only secret: get the best help you can, and enough of it!

Remember, when necessary, send your material out first to be hot-washed to take out the shrinkage before you start to cut anything.

SPECIALTY MANUFACTURE:

Includes silkscreen, vacuform, latex, metalwork, castings, embroidery, and all the non-traditional sewing machine manufacture that might help you build your costumes.

These craftspeople usually advertise in the Yellow Pages, online, and in trade magazines. Printing your own material, making your own armor or other special skill work will mean that, unless you have access to the talent directly, you will be hiring these peoples' businesses. Searching out new areas for local costume labor, you might also look for help from: costume shops; college theater departments; civic operas; or neighborhood live theaters.

There are several pages of business and personal ads in the "411" book or other industry-related directories (available at larger newsstands or bookstores, see Reference — Chapter 21).

135

Bo Hopkins
Shaughnessy

chapter **15**

ASSEMBLING THE COSTUMES

Wherever your department is, in town or on location, you have to set up the stock clothing. Even when you're pulling the clothes from a costume house, you have to assemble them according to some system of organization that allows you to "see" your show and work it without losing anything.

I first separate a section for Men and Women. In each section I allow rack space for the development of Cast clothing and Featured Bits. Then comes the general stock, again by men's and women's, with boys and girls at the end of each. I then separate everything within each group by type: daywear, evening dress, sport, character, ethnic, service uniform, and military uniform. Sometimes, these divisions are by "set," if the sets call for distinct costumes.

The way you assemble your stock is the way you'll keep it through shooting. Remember, you're assembling parts for your wardrobe machine; you want to make sure you have what you want and you know where it is, when you need it.

As you keep the clothes by set and type, you can see what goes with what — it's the closest thing you'll have for a rehearsal. Lining up the clothes by set, you can see what needs to be over-dyed, where you might want some more color or character, size range, or accessories.

By lining up the characters' clothing, part by part, you can see the balance, color, and types against each other.

All these reasons and more will conclude the next chapter on fittings.

When working on location off a large truck, I try and keep the "working" clothes on the lower racks and the "extra stock" on the upper ones. As we change sets I rearrange the stock, again, putting the current "working stock" low. "Dead" cast clothing (clothing that has worked) is kept together, by change, in plastic garment bags, tagged with the character name, and working scene number — again, up high and out of the way. I never put actor' names on anything, too tempting a target for souvenir hunters.

Now that you have your clothing in hand, you can get ready for the next hurdle — cast fittings and the "Show-and-Tell" that will follow.

JACKSON &
WIFE.

139

Kali Rocha and Stephen Lang
Gods and Generals

THE WIND AND THE LION
TEDDY ROOSVELT

Costume for Brian Keith
The Wind and the Lion

chapter **16**

FITTING THE ACTOR: SHOW-AND-TELL

The next big stage of getting a show on the road is fitting the actors and having them approved with a "Show-and-Tell" or "Show-and-Yell," as we used to call them.

ACTORS:

There are as many situations as there are actors and shows; a few are inexperienced, insecure, and demanding; some are laid back and easy; many are highly intelligent and very thoughtful. Again, most have seen your job done by someone else, perhaps many times.

Best-case scenario — You love and admire each other and each other's work. You create together, in an atmosphere of support and trust. to develop a mutual artistic vision whose dazzling brightness sparkles in the imagination of all. Worst-case scenario — They complain, demean, and embarrass you, and finally argue hysterically over some nonsensical, never-discussed, trivial item and get you fired.

In other words, there can be lots of ego... but, what do you expect? These are people who have to expose and display their fears, insecurities, and vulnerabilities to large and uncaring audiences for a living. Most of the time, they respond to a sound design plan, and to the security of knowing that they will be cared for; that they are receiving the benefit of *your* expertise and concern in assembling the costume tools from which they will fashion their characters. Some are more collaborative than others. In general, the higher on the cast sheet, the more they are allowed to demand. Then again, the higher on the cast sheet, the more secure and the least demanding. Be prepared. Be secure. Have a plan. Be gracious and flexible.

Modern shows are, sometimes, harder than period shows. The reason is simple — on period shows, most will defer to the Costume Designer, as long as everything "looks" right. On modern shows, everyone's the expert. Everyone has opinions and some are thinking about what they will be wearing home *after* the show.

★Years ago at Fox, they told me: "Never be friends with actors." The idea was to always be friendly, but never try and be friends. The reason was that actors had full lives, too. They might desire camaraderie on the set, but they are not there to be your buddies. Professionalism dictates that you always be gracious with them but respect a professional, personal, and social distance that allows them the freedom to withdraw mentally, when they have to, and that you never, never bug them with personal junk on the set. I found that to always be good advice. You're a professional Designer, not a star groupie or valet, no matter how impressed you are to be with them (and sometimes it's pretty impressive).

This seems like a natural moment to say a little about the history of star fittings and a Costume Designer whom just about everyone has heard of... Edith Head.

Back in the roaring '20s, costumes were designed by men like Adrian or Erte. Designers who came from the world of stage, opera, silent films. The costumes were, almost always, somewhat over scale and "grand," not to say flamboyant.

Edith started in the '30s, with the rise of sound and big studio productions and big studio "Stars."

Edith helped invent the concept of "Star Wardrobe," merging fashion with contemporary clothes with costume fantasy, putting the focus of her work on making the star look great on film. By her own admission she was the "queen of camouflage" who would assess everyone the same way in the fitting room: What were their good points and how to emphasize them, at the same time taking attention away from any "bad" or awkward points, and she always tried to do it with the simplest of lines. She designed a lot of classic clothes following those rules, and this is the point of the "Tailor's" fitting — to adjust the clothes so they (within the scope of the drama) flatter the star, whenever possible with the cut and fit.

While Edith is remembered as a much-celebrated Designer, there were, and are, many others.

In the '30s, the era of the Studio System, there was a lot of prep time and a reasonable amount of money to get the stars on screen. There were legendary partnerships between some Designers and some stars: Orry-Kelly and Bette Davis; Cecil Beaton and Marlene Dietrich. The '50s brought Travilla and Marilyn Monroe, and from the world of fashion, Givenchy and Audrey Hepburn; more recently, Bob Mackie and Cher.

To a large degree, these Designers were looking to create a "fantasy" image. Today, the films are less glamorous and more "real" and seem to call for more real-looking clothing.

There are, of course, many talented Designers working today, too many for me to recount; I ask their understanding.

Another story: years ago, Mom (from the old school), instructed me on how to go about making dresses for an actress, basing her advice on the studio system that she had spent years in: "First, do your research, get photos from history books that get you close to the right "look," then do a concept sketch and swatch everything. Find a dress in stock that comes close to what you want. Put the sample garment on a dress form and sketch it. Staple the swatches to the sketch. Go to the Camera Department, have them photograph the drawing and material with the film stock that they're going to shoot the film with and put the photo with the drawing; then go to the head cutter/fitter, have her do a yardage count on the fabric you want and get it priced. Finally, check with the ladies wardrobe department supervisor to see if the proper foundation garments exist or have to be made, also. Then prepare all the dress-change drawings in the same way for a "Show-and-Tell" with the producer and director, where you can discuss the "look," all the manufacture and its prices."

143

As beautiful and professional a system as that once was, I know that I've never had the time to even think about doing that much ground work on things that had to be made (although the steps, as an ideal to try for, are great to know).

My often-regurgitated point is that the business has changed. It's harder now to do the kind of work that those brilliant Designers of yesterday did for a few reasons: First, lack of time and money. Today, all but the biggest features are shot with slim budgets. This means less prep time and less manufacture. Which means more reliance on the rental of "stock" items. Second, "stock" at costume houses is not replaced with any regularity and you might find that your show, when rented, is a mixture of first and second choices, at least where the background is concerned.

That's the importance of limited manufacture and the tailor fitting with leading cast members. These are the people who will be telling the story, who will have most of the screen time and will be featured in large, 20-foot-high shots — this is the place to spend time and money. Remember: If you don't take the time to do things correctly in the beginning, when will you have time to fix them later?

THE FITTING PROCESS:

The process goes something like this:

1). Casting provides you with the name and contact information of an actor who will play a leading part. You're familiar with that part from all your readings of the script — now you have a face to put with it. How does this casting reality affect your thinking?

2). You see if any costume houses have the actors' sizes on file from *recent* fittings. If not, call casting and try and get the contacts of the actors' agents, management companies, or personal secretaries. In any event, call the actors personally, introduce yourself and get sizes, head to toe. Have written questions waiting and fill in the blanks — height, weight, head or hat size, neck, sleeve, bust or chest, (dress size), waist, hip, outseam, inseam, shoe size. Ask the actors their thoughts about the parts (characters) and if any clothes had been made recently by anyone you can contact (for current sizes and possible manufacture use) — and, note everything! Then schedule a time to see them. Most of the time, they will come to the fitting room, but sometimes you have to go to their homes or hotel rooms — either way, the process will be the same.

Many times people will underestimate their sizes... call it vanity or wishful thinking — they almost *always* err on the small side.

Whenever possible, I like to have a first fitting with an actor alone, that is, with just the fitting-room help, costumers, and tailor. The reason for this is that I want some private time with the actor to start a relationship — to get his or her feelings for the part and the clothes, and to work out any problems together. Done this way, when the "Show-and-Tell" happens, the actor will help sell the clothes he or she is comfortable with — that is *very* helpful.

144

Scheduling actor fittings takes some thought also — try not to cram too many fittings into one day, unless there aren't many changes. If it's the first fitting and you have lots of things to try on, always allow a little more time than you think you need between fittings. If your first fitting is late, your whole day is a mess.

If you have reasonable preparation time and have clothes to make, you might have two or more fittings. If you're on location and an actor who works the next day comes in, then you better have a good system and extra clothing ready and waiting.

FITTING THE ACTOR:

There are different kinds of fittings: The first one is a trial fitting where you usually try to use some rented and/or purchased clothing, while you measure for correct sizes in preparation for the manufacture (M.O.) of selected pieces. This is where you and the actor talk "part," you show your research, samples, sketches, and swatches and set up a working relationship.

If you're making clothes, plan for the second fitting that is a natural outgrowth of the tailor-shop process; before finishing, the actor tries the clothes on so that the fit can be checked for final adjustments/alterations. This may be when new purchases are tried on, also, for a first look at the intended change.

145

You will want to photograph the fittings with special attention to close-up shots, remembering that when the actor will be filmed, much of it will be in close-up for dialogue... how does that collar, tie, hat or anything else around the face look? No matter about the great job you did finding and getting all the fantastic-looking clothes for everyone else, if the actor in close-up is ill fitted the rest doesn't mean much. Those fitting photos can be sent to the director to keep production appraised of progress.

There's another kind of fitting. It happens when the costumes are assembled in your department, on location. Everything has been discussed and approved by the director *before* the actor was hired. You have selected choices for each change, for each actor, which hang — waiting. Then, the actors come in a day or two before shooting begins. They see their clothes for the first time. Maybe they don't like them. Maybe they want to wear something else — that's the fitting we want to look at now.

It will happen on every show. All the preliminary discussion about wardrobe, costume changes, specific character looks, will be done with the director, producer, production designer, everyone but the person who will be asked to wear them. What if that person has other ideas?

To be sure, in most cases you will enjoy some contact with the leading actors before the shoot. You should have the opportunity to exchange ideas on their roles and arrive at something you both can live with. Many actors, seasoned professionals who are cast late, know the futility of demanding too much attention or specific wardrobe. But, of course, they all have their own ideas about what they're doing and how best to illustrate it.

What I'm going to assert now is true. In 40 years of dressing actors (in the hundreds), I haven't had a dozen outfits changed on the set, and not too many changed at the fittings. Is it because I'm great? Not at all. It's because I was taught a great system that works.

Let's say you're on that show. You've had all the concept meetings, you have your research, you're ready... and you start getting cast. Now, all actors who come in for fittings will be wanting to protect themselves, and rightfully so. They might not know anyone on the show. They may be insecure about their looks. They may have done their own research. But, naturally, they will want to look "their best," at least as far as their characters are concerned.

How do you set up the fitting so that the clothes *you* like will be the clothes *they* like?

By this time, when actors start to come in, you have had some weeks of prep. Think of your breakdown sheets, cast and background. This is why we group the clothes together **by cast part** and **by set** (type). This is why I try and hang the costumes together in the order that they will be used. "The Saloon," "The Indian Village," "The Funeral." I do this so that I can see them together. So that every group develops its own integrity. So that department costumers can learn the "looks" and so that costume units can be "tweaked" by group, after all, that's how they're going to appear on screen and this is as close to a costume rehearsal as you will get.

I then assemble the cast clothing by actor — a couple of options for each change; search them out, sort them out, hang them together. Know what change will work where. At this time, if I can't find something for the actor to wear, I try and find samples that are close in cut

146

or style, regardless of size or color. I put these samples in their order with swatches of the fabric intended for the new manufacture, so the actor can see the proposed garments and the tailor can discuss them at the coming fitting.

I try to integrate *everything* I know about the character, everything I've felt from reading the script, everything I've seen in research, everything I've heard in meetings, everything I've found or made according to everything I believe as a Costume Illustrator. I then check the character changes against each other — if they appear in the scene together — to be sure they work together and express the dramatic intent of the scene or inter-character relationship. By this time you have already checked with the production designer about the specific set colors that will be the background for the costumes. *Then* call the actor in for a fitting with the tailor. No one else, if possible.

When the actors arrive, I try to be as friendly and relaxed as I can (sometimes not easy). I start with the research... show them period illustrations and design sketches. I explain the concept, show the color chips and swatches... then move to the clothes, group by group, set by set. I try and show the actors what will surround them, give them a sense of scale, a sense of thoroughness. Then on to the cast clothes. This is the "Good Guy," this is the "Bad Guy." This is the "Leading Lady" — this is her change when you meet her for the first time. **These are your clothes.** It's essential to give the actors a sense of comfort. You *want* them to be at ease in your clothes. You want them to feel free to be their characters and not distracted by worry that they "don't look right." They have to both, "fit in" and "stand out."

The best way to do this is to show them that they are part of a larger design and within that design, their costumes have their own attention points that create a visual illustration of *their* characters that they can relax in, take comfort from, and even be inspired and strengthened by.

Now, you and the actors can find the "gags" in their outfits, things they can work with. Hats they can push around on their heads, handkerchiefs they can mop their foreheads with, bags they can clutch nervously, things that will help them "sell their characters" in the scenes to come.

Frequently, character costumes are strengthened by "signature" pieces. A signature piece can be anything — a hat, tie, jewelry, scarf, shoulder pads, a color scheme, a tight "look" or a baggy shirt... something that "nails" the character and stays the same or repeats, even though other parts of the costumes change. A signature piece truly "defines" the character, while the rest of the costume changes are a function of time or circumstance.

If actors walk into the dressing room without the benefit of knowing or trusting you, or knowing what the show will look like, you can't blame them for being defensive or wanting what they want. My experience is that when actors are comfortable with the clothes, they will be your biggest allies.

There are other ways to do it that are less self-assertive and more collaborative. Everything stays the same, except, in addition to selecting actor's changes, you select everything you can that might constitute the character's wardrobe closets. When the actor comes in for the fitting, you show "the closet," then try on this-and-that, scene by scene, until you arrive at something that the actor is comfortable with. This can be a better way to work with some "stars." They are smart people and most of the time know what works for them, but it can lead to a laundry-list of accessories to shop.

Stylists sometimes have to work like this on commercials and videos where the client/producer may also be the star and where the director, agency representatives, and art director may expect lots of input on the "look." This can create a design-by-committee situation where the stylist has to bring **lots** of choices to the fittings. This works well on smaller, talent-centered projects, or even larger star-centered, modern shows, where you can shop your way out. But, on a large period show that demands manufacture or where there is limited stock available, it can result in a loss of design focus. It also can cause you to have to adjust a large cast around one player, taking up lots of time and money that's in short supply.

★I have worked mostly on costume films and, with the preproduction clock ticking, always want the most efficient use of my time and money, So, I favor constructing a strong sense of design options with color and costumes that I can get approved by production and show the actors when they come in for the first time. I feel it's good to establish a "show reality" that everyone is comfortable with and we can all work within. Find out early how your production company sees the process happening and whom they will want to be there, if anyone.

There's another situation that sometimes arises. Let's say that you've done all the prep work and selected the costume changes. Then, the actor walks in, and you know at a glance, that everything you picked is wrong.

Sometimes, no matter how good your design concept, you realize that you hadn't **seen** the actor before; and now that you do, you know that the clothes are not going to work on that person. Graciousness and flexibility are the key. If you are surrounded by your whole department, you can undoubtedly find something, at least to get started.

Try to never lose control of your fitting. Apologize. Bring the actor into the process... "I thought this would be good for your character... but now that I see you, I'm not sure. What do you think?" Work together. I believe that the actor will be impressed enough by your concern, frankness, and willingness to find the "right" thing, that he or she will gladly help brainstorm a character session with you, and together, something wonderful can happen.

Sometimes you will have a first choice... and someone will want another thing, see another dress or tie, and like it better. Some designers are disappointed at not having their first choices accepted. Is the second thing a bad choice? The reality is that anything that anyone picks all comes out of the costume stock that you've selected... they're all your choices... be happy.

One last thing. Sometimes, there are storms at sea. Sometimes, arguments, dissatisfactions, misunderstandings, insecurities, dark and violent things that you have no knowledge of, manifest themselves at the moment of truth known as the "fitting."

One moment you're the happy sailor, confidently piloting your small craft across a calm sea, then — Hurricane Evil blows in — bringing chaos and destruction; everything is in shambles, the decks are awash with blood. You're back in the fitting room alone, clothes are everywhere, you're trying to remember what everyone was yelling about. Wow! Well, we've all been there. It was nothing personal.

The thing **now** is Damage Control. Graciousness and flexibility. What must you mend to get back underway? Consider doing nothing and letting the situation blow over, then try again to make it happen. People will respect you for it.

149

Once everything is set, a real "Show-and-Tell" with the director is desirable. In fact, during the beginning phases of preparation I'm always building toward the Show-and-Tell meeting. The reasons for this are simple: 1) Common courtesy. When hired, we work for production, and it's our job to give them the show that they want (sometimes better). Whether or not your view of a costume is at odds with the director's or producer's, you owe them a meeting, showing and explaining all things before shooting. Answer questions and work out kinks before you get to the set; 2) Professional attention. Much the same reason. After all, it's a collaboration and this is the time-honored way that things happen before production. Sometimes the clothes are hanging when viewed, sometimes it's a "costume parade" with one or more actors wearing their changes for production to see; 3) Personal satisfaction. You've worked hard during prep to accumulate and fit your costumes — be proud of them, show them off. If you are at odds with production about a concept or character, nothing will help you more than a confident display of your reasons.

This is also a prime opportunity to show off your department. Up until now, your relationship with production has mostly been in small meetings or on the phone. They've never really seen what you've been doing and many times don't appreciate the volume of costumes you will have to handle or the size of your shop, or its contribution to their show. All they know is that they have been asked to pay for it. Well, now's your time to show them everything. The look of the background, set by set, other cast members, special items, made items. Show them that you're prepared and that they will have a great-looking show. Chances are they will come away with a new appreciation for you and your department and everyone can march into shooting together with confidence and optimism.

P.S.: Don't forget, a good final fitting, and/or Show-and-Tell will involve the property master. Some prop people won't be as keen as others, but if they're willing and available, it's always good to see the costumes with the jewelry, canes, guns, glasses, and other hand props that will help create the character.

This approach will have dividends later on, too — on the set. If everyone has seen and approved of the costumes ahead of time, then there are no surprises. People feel comfortable with what they see and you're much less likely to hear things like: "I didn't know she was going to wear that!" or "I hate this outfit!" or the infamous "I'm not going to wear that @3$%^&★ thing!" — words guaranteed to upset your stomach.

Now that you have your cast fitted and your background pulled, it's time to address getting it all to look right with aging and distressing.

Japanese pilot
Research sketch, *Pearl Harbor*

chapter **17**

AGING
AND
DISTRESSING

What does this mean? Well, it means giving a piece of costume character. It means taking a new piece and making it look old and worn — "real." There are no set rules for this process but some methods work better than others — you have to be willing to experiment and get dirty, but it's worth it. No matter how you choose to try, you probably will use the same supplies, so let's go over the most important ones. Before we go any further, a cautionary note. Aging and distressing can ruin clothing. Be sure you know who **owns** the clothes you're working on and whether you're allowed to damage the clothes or not. By damage I mean making holes or using color that will not come out. This is especially true if you're using authentic and original clothing from a rental house. Remember, these old pieces have survived over time, and are now ready to support you on your show because of the care that a generation or more of costume people have given them. Please, don't destroy them out of lack of respect or through carelessness.

COMMERCIAL SAND / STONE / ACID-WASH PLACES:
These are very good and fast methods for really breaking down lots of clothes in a hurry, but you must use caution. If the laundry doesn't use a bleach arrester on the final cycle, your clothes will look fine when you get them, but further washing or exposure to the sun may bleach them past where you want to go.

If you're working on a smaller scale, try experimenting with fabric softener, bleach, and color remover; but experiment on extra costumes or pieces of fabric. The first step is to soften the fabric and remove all the loose color (the color that will come out with a few washings).

The second step is to paint or over-dye the garments in an uneven fashion to resemble ground-in dirt. If you own the clothes and don't care, use diluted paint if you like, but if the clothes are rented, use Fullers Earth (which can be bought at any costume house) with mineral oil, water, or dry. Rental houses take a dim view of returning their clothes with paint on them and you will surely pay.

When doing a medium-size job on location, I mix a bath of Fullers Earth and water with a little brown dye, put it onto a large galvanized tub and give the garments a bath, then hang them on double hangers in the sun and squirt them from the top down with water and a little bleach, letting the sun do the rest.

The third step is the "ragging." This can be done with anything from scissors and razor blades, to fish scalars and sandpaper, to beating holes into the fabric with a hammer on concrete or asphalt.

I've known people who have thrown new clothes into a rented cement mixer with loose gravel or bricks.

SUPPLIES:

Fullers Earth: this in a very fine, sifted powder that can be purchased at any costume rental house (and some paint stores). Fullers Earth is the generic name for all colored, sifted earth, but it also refers to a specific color: Fullers Earth is a dark taupe color. **Rottenstone** is lighter, looks like concrete powder. **Burnt Umber** is very dark brown. **Raw Umber** has a red cast to it. **Lamp Black** is just that, black. You can also find these powders in **Red Oxide** and **Raw** or **Burnt Sienna**. These powders are very fine and because of that, they get into everything, if not used with caution. *Never* use them in a room where things have to be kept clean, or on a table that will be used as a cutting table. If used with the right vehicle, these powders are a dry pigment for mixing paint.

A "Grease Rag" is used all the time and is made with the same powders. You can apply them with various mediums, water, Lexol, mineral oil, alcohol, in other words, just about anything. Mineral oil is favored because of the easy spread and speed of application. A piece of terry cloth is soaked with oil, then filled with earth and "smushed around" until the surface of the rag is covered by the dark paste combination. The rag is then rolled and kept in a plastic zip bag until needed. The rag can be wiped around cuffs, collars, elbows, knees, anywhere you want dirt to show. For subtler use, use your fingers after wiping them on the grease rag.

I'm not sure what the Volatile Organic Compounds (VOC) rating is, but it's probably not good. All this powder should be used wearing protective gloves, mask, and eye wear.

(*Volatile Organic Compounds* — new Federal health rules subject everything to standard minimum guidelines — check everything that goes next to the body!)

POUNCE BAGS:

Made with the same powders. The powder is poured into a white gym sock and the open end taped shut. The powder will sift out through the material or "brush" on dry to clothing.

In the "old days," we used to fold cheese cloth into squares about 18" x 18" — three or four layers thick — heap powder in the center — fold up the corners and tape together, around the top. Gym socks are easier. The powder can be "dusted" on anything.

HAIR SPRAY:

Comes in various colors. Can be diluted with water by spritzing into streaks or modeled with a damp rag or sponge. Works great on slippery surfaces like straw hats and plastic slickers/ponchos. Hard to get out after drying.

LEATHER SPRAY:

Comes in a great variety of colors, made to change the color of leather. It's dye — hard to get out.

HOUSE PAINT:

Either spray or liquid, has many and varied uses — can create a wide variety of finishes and textures.

SPRITZ BOTTLES:

Hudson sprayers and Flachettes are for spraying a controlled amount of water on your work surface. Can be used to spray dye or water, "dirtied" with Fullers Earth.

SAND PAPER:

For breaking down fabric or leather.

OIL:

Lexol and mineral oil are my two favorites. Either use by themselves or in combination with Fullers Earth.

OTHER TOOLS:

Limited only by your imagination —
Anything sharp; for breaking holes in the fabric.
Anything blunt; for beating holes in the fabric.
Blow torch or propane torch for singeing fabric.

156

Note: Western Costume Company has its own line of aging products. You can check with their supply store for information: (818) 760-0900.

AGING TECHNIQUES:

Let's start with hats. When doing a Western, the hat is everything. When fitting extras, we'll fit the hat first, find the one that really works with the face, then dress the rest of the outfit, accordingly. I always like to take a lot of hats that have a "natural" shape, that is, the crown is fully rounded without creases, and shape it to the actor's face during the fitting, but the big thing is breaking it down, especially a new hat.

The easiest way is a little dangerous (for the hat) — fill a bucket with water and bleach. The more bleach you use, the stronger the solution and the faster the action. Given enough time, a full bleach solution will "eat" a hat to pieces, so a gentle soak in a 50/50 solution will work slowly enough for you to keep tabs on it. The bleach will eat off the nap and thin the "hand" or body of the felt, soften it, as well as take out the color.

If you don't want to take it down that far, use shaving cream and a safety razor and shave the hat. You will preserve the color, but by taking off the nap, the hat will start looking worn.

You can work outside with a spritz bottle of water and bleach, squirting the hat and letting the sun help.

To help it keep its shape, we always used to soak the hat in beer and water (an old cowboy trick), then shape it by hand and set it in the sun to dry. When the hat dries, the beer impregnates the felt and leaves it stiff, keeping the hat shape. You can use "Hat Sizing," which is made for the job, but it's not as romantic. If it's a straw hat, squirt it first, overall, with water, then lightly spray it with brown hair spray from about a foot away. When the brown looks like you've made a mistake, spritz it again with water. The brown tint will "slide" on the water and look like rain streaks. You can dab at it with a sponge or paper towel also — this will further mottle the color. In fact, as long as you keep it wet, you will be able to get rid of most, if not all of the brown tint. When you have it where you want it, fix it with a shot of "dulling" spray or "matt" varnish.

Working with a felt hat? Dark hats are very forgiving, but light-colored hats can retain mistakes, so go slowly.

For larger jobs, or more permanent results, you need to start with a large, sunlit outside area. I always try to buy a galvanized "horse feeder" or large laundry tub. Fill the tub with water and Fullers Earth. Heat a pan of water and dissolve a couple of packages of tan dye, then add this to the Fullers Earth mixture. Stir the pot — then dunk the clothes, wring them out slightly and hang them on double wooden hangers. I like to drape an old bath towel around the hanger first, this way the shoulder of the garment is softened at the edges and doesn't pick up hanger marks... you also can throw things on the ground to dry, turning them over to the sun.

On *Gods and Generals*, another costumer and I dirtied 400 soldiers in overcoats each morning, in the time it took them to walk past us. We set up a horse feeder with Fullers Earth and water, stood on either side of it with wide wallpaper brushes and had the soldiers line up in front of us. As they walked past us, we slopped the bottoms of their overcoats as they went to the set.

If you want a new garment to look old and droopy, cover a dress form with a trash bag and hang the garment on the form. Put rocks in the pockets and get it wet. Now you can spritz the top shoulder area, chest, center back, and outer arms with a mixture of bleach and water to create some fading. The aging looks more natural if it's done this way, because of the body shape of the form, especially at the shoulder area.

157

Want to take it down a little more? While wet, the fabric will give differently — so now, hit the edges of the garment with a rasp, file, fish scaler, anything to break the fabric weave.

For a little extra character, look around elbows and knees, find some fabric you like... and patch the elbow or knee hole from underneath. You can also use other fabric to bind the edges of lapels or cuffs. If you are adding patches, age them as you go so they look like the rest of the garment. If the patches are unaged, the garment will have a "Raggedy Ann," clownish look (maybe that's what you want).

Leather items are another story. If you're aging newly made leather clothing, a bath in a tub of Fuller's and water will soften the color and give it a more "natural" look, and it will accept aging from a grease rag, also. You can wash and dry a new leather garment a couple of times before you ruin it. But, if you're starting from scratch, you should go directly to a tannery and get the leather before they finish it with a "natural" finish. Sometimes, they call it a simulated smoked or brain-tanned finish. (Find them online).

158

If you have to use leather that already has a "Chromate" finish and are making period or ethnic costumes where you want a natural look, you might have to have the leather sandblasted first, in order to break down the factory finish and open the leather to taking your dye and aging.

If you're trying to age a modern-made leather garment, coat, pants, chaps, etc., get ready for a time-consuming and dirty process.

You first have to take the factory protective finish off the leather. This can be done with Leather Preparer, acetone, lacquer thinner or paint remover (always wear gloves) and a rag (On *Last of the Mohicans*, we had so much leather, and the hides were so big, we would staple the cow hides to a piece of plywood and sandblast the chromate finish off).

Once the finish has been removed, areas that have to show more use can then be sanded down deeper into the raw leather.

From here on it's up to the kind of finish that you're going after. The leather can be mottled with color using alcohol-based leather dyes. A finish can be painted on, then sealed. Lacquer or varnish can stiffen and look "crystallized." The best way is to leave yourself open and have something extra that you can experiment with.

★Tip: When aging clothing with unfamiliar materials, check out samples first. I've seen shows that tried to use spray cooking oil for fast results to simulate sweat, not realizing that the oil would go rancid and really smell bad later. I remember a show that tried to get dirty sweat marks on cast clothing using liquid shoe polish, only to find that when combined with the actor's real sweat it begin to sting him in soft skin areas — he refused to wear the clothes, and since **all** his costumes were aged the same way, a whole new wardrobe had to be found overnight. Bleach can sometimes stay in the garments and cause the same problem. Make sure the costumes you age are wearable!

By this stage, most everything has been sent to location or developed in your department space. The Supervisor has hired the crew, you've all had a few weeks to work together and you're facing the next step... Shooting!

Aide for General Jackson
Gods and Generals

chapter **18**

THE SHOOT

The primary objective of the department during the production phase is supplying costumes for the camera according to the shooting schedule; all the design and department preparation work is aimed at this objective — getting everything in front of the camera to be photographed. While this is a book about Costume Design, I realize that you might be hired as "Designer," with little or no help, so, I'm going to try and describe an average shooting day and its duties. Because everybody is working at the same time, I'm going to follow one job for a while, then back up and discuss another.

For a Supervisor, a normal location day might be something like this: You start at 4:30 a.m. or 5:00 a.m., load your crew out of their motel rooms and into the department car or van for your drive to the set. When I was crew, I took this opportunity to sleep; when I was supervising, I took this opportunity to talk the day's schedule over with the Designer and/or Key. We would map out a plan for our labor. What was on the call sheet for the day? What department work had to be done? What did we still have to do to prep an upcoming scene? When we got to the location and opened the truck we had a pretty good idea of what to do first.

The two main jobs on any morning are: Getting the extras dressed and to the set; Getting the actors' dressing rooms set up with the right clothes for their first changes.

The shooting crew isn't here yet, just some drivers, maybe a second assistant director, someone from casting with the extras, hair and make-up people, it may be too early even for the catering truck.

COSTUME DESIGN 101 / 2ND EDITION / *Richard La Motte*

The **Key Set Person** goes straight for the cast clothing. We always used the last rack in the truck on the right hand side for cast clothing. We put their clothing on the high racks for storage; this was to keep principal clothes out of reach and sight for anyone who was not in the department, and also to keep the dead storage up and out of the way.

Next to the Supervisor, the Key Set Person is the most **important** person on your crew. Why? Simple. He or she is your department's direct representative on the set with the actors, continuity, camera, first assistant director and director. You and your department will be perceived through the actions, dependability, personality, competence, concern, helpfulness and all around professionalism of this person. This person is the "eyes and ears" of your department on the set. This person will receive any set-conceived changes in schedule, cast or anything else, first. This person will be in a position of close personal contact with every actor. This person will be responsible for keeping continuity with the script supervisor, keeping the "set book" up to date, and keeping track of many thousands of dollars worth of, perhaps irreplaceable, cast clothing. As far as experience is concerned, I would give anyone a chance to do the job, for the first time, if he or she wanted it badly enough to take it seriously, possessed the alertness, and understood professional set behavior. In fact, I would rather have that new person than someone who had done it a thousand times and didn't care or was lazy or distracted.

On a new location, we would check with the second AD as to where the rooms were for each actor. It's production's job to assign dressing rooms and trailers. When we knew which actors were in which rooms, we would bring over the clothes and set up.

*We always were taught to hang the actor's change individually in clear plastic garment bags — footwear with the costume, with a loop of string, at the bottom of the hanging outfit; this takes about six to eight feet on the double. The reason? You keep the outfit together, wherever it hangs, whenever it's moved. Why hang shoes low? So shoe polish won't get on the clothes and you can see them to make sure they're there, especially when on their way to the actor's dressing room. It also lets you keep your hands free when carrying more than one outfit. Plastic Shoe Bags? Unless dropped on a string, they make multiple outfits too bulky to carry.

162

Setting up actors: Only put the clothes in the room that work, or that you want them to wear. If you put extra clothes in their rooms, even hidden in the closet, you will, one day, find cast members wandering around in their own clothes asking "What do I wear." When you tell them that you put their first change out and the later change in the closet, they will tell you that it confused them. The other thing they taught us was to lay the change out in a mistake-proof fashion; that is, put the tie around the collar, put the cuff-links in the shirt, put the belt in the pants, put the socks on top of the shoes. Lay everything out neatly so that the actor has only to put the change on and not think about it.

With period shows your cast women will need help with under-garments and dresses.

If the actors have a lot of make up to get into, provide them with T-shirts, or foundation garments and robes, letting them get into their costumes after make up, thereby saving the collars.

Take to the set what you don't think the actor will wear, overcoat, hat, gloves, etc. If you take them to the set, it will save you from running back to get them later.

Extras: If we knew we had a big "extra" day coming, we would always try for a pre-fit day, fitting all the extras and having any alterations done in advance. Sometimes that's not possible, for one reason or another. If we can't get the extras ahead of time, and the sizes are generic (Arab, Native American, primitive) we try to put up outfits, by size, in advance, this way, you can keep the pieces that you like together, and see that they go out as outfits.

There are several ways to try and control extra crowds, that is, create a system that promotes order and helps you re-capture the clothes as efficiently as possible.

One way is to use sign-out sheets. Sign-out sheets can be any size. We used to have them about 18" x 24" but you can make them any size you want. Number down the left hand margin. If you have 100 extras, then you need 100 numbered lines. When the extras come for clothes the **first** time, write down their names and make out tags with corresponding numbers. Those numbers are **their** numbers for the show. You take their pay vouchers, write their numbers on them and file them in a box. When

163

the extras are fitted, they are told to "go to the dressing area, put on your costume, hang your clothes on the hanger, or put them in a shoe or laundry bag, pin **your** numbered tag to your clothes, and bring your clothes back to the wardrobe area."

When they return with their clothes, tagged with their numbers, you hang their personal clothes in consecutive order in your department. This way, during the day, they can't take off with your clothes and their clothes, too. At the end of the day, you reverse the process, they come to the department, retrieve their clothes by number, change, return their costumes with their numbered tags on the sleeves. If they return complete, you give them back their pay vouchers, hang their outfits in the department, in consecutive order, and hope that tomorrow morning they will remember their numbers.

You will want to have laundry bags waiting at the truck to receive their socks, T-shirts, stockings, whatever is washable, overnight. There are many variations on this system. Sometimes they leave their personal clothes on racks in the changing area. Sometimes you will want to write down the items that constitute their outfits; however you do it, the reason is the same... control the clothes.

You will be amazed that people can find so many ways to put clothes on hangers. In other parts of the world costumers use large mesh laundry bags to hold personal clothing rather than hanging things up.

We always found that it's best to have someone circulate in the dressing area while the extras are getting changed as it does a couple of things: You're able to help those who need help, and by so doing, establish a rapport with them in general and, your presence helps deter those light-fingered souvenir hunters. The same is true for the line of extras returning costumes to the truck. Someone should walk the line offering hangers, pins and help in getting their outfits ready to be received... it saves a lot of time at the truck when everybody wants to go home, after a long day. This working in proximity to people dressing and undressing can be uncomfortable for folks not used to it — for that reason I always hire costume men and women to work with extra crowds of the same gender, it speeds the process and saves embarrassment. Children must have a separate boy/girl area and it's law that you cannot issue clothing worn next to the body, from one person to the next, without washing it.

BACK TO THE SET:

As a Key Set Person, I would always check first with the first AD and make sure that the call sheet, issued the night before, was still good and reflected the order that they planned to shoot that day. Sometimes ideas are thought up after the call sheet comes out and you won't know the changes unless you ask.

If the AD told me that they had added shots from another day that weren't on the call sheet, I would check the matching notes in my set book, then let the Supervisor know what the changes were, so the truck crew could make sure that the costumes needed were available and not at the cleaners or being repaired or being stored off the location.

They always told me that the best set people were the ones who understood that the job consisted of two parts: 1) Keeping track of, and working, the cast clothing to camera, and 2) Constantly keeping ahead of the company with information. This means always finding out what the company is going to shoot next, and keeping the department notified so that the department is never caught flat-footed and is always in a position to get a jump on preparing for an upcoming changed scene.

I would always check with the camera operator as to what was in frame and they always let me look for myself. This gave me a realistic idea as to what the camera saw, and I would know better what to do, accordingly.

First day of shooting, I would always check in with the script supervisor and compare breakdowns. We always wanted to make sure that our breakdowns matched, with regard to how many "story days" there were and that the "day breaks" were at the same scene numbers. The script supervisor matched everything in the scene except wardrobe (sometimes some did, especially if a wardrobe "gag" was happening as part of the action) They would always tell me, "Look, I have too much to keep track of already, you have to match the clothes." I would have anyway, that's what the department had me there for.

At the start of the day, I would sit with the call sheet and set book and figure out which actors would have to change clothes during the day, for which scenes and what the changes were. I would line up those changes on the truck or trailer to make sure that they were there, then go to the set. During the day, when I saw that we were getting close to the scene in which the actor was to change, I would tell the first AD, so he or she would know to break them. When they did break, I would go set up the next change. After the actor had changed, I would collect the last change, making sure that it was all there, and return it to the department. I was always told to *never* leave clothes unattended in a an unlocked trailer (That's not the same if you're using a Honey Wagon, where the driver is always close. Remember, at the wrap, those drivers are in a hurry to leave and will want you to get those rooms empty as fast as possible.)

I would try and take things like actors' coats and hats to the set, least they arrive without them after make-up — requiring me to run to their trailers to get their missing pieces. I would do this also when lunch was called, because sometimes actors can get busy and leave their things on the backs of chairs, or elsewhere.

We always had rolling clothing racks at the studio on stage, so I always had a portable department to keep anything that wasn't being worn. Out in the field, where little rack wheels won't go, I always borrowed a "C" stand from my grip brothers for a stationary place to hang clothes, always making sure of returning it (right to their truck, if I could).

When the director got to the set, I would always say "good morning" and stand close enough to hear the director lay out the shots with the first assistant and cameraman.

When I was satisfied that there weren't going to be any changes, I would turn my attention to the actors who were getting to the set from make-up, making sure that they had their outfits, hadn't left anything in their rooms or the make-up department.

The next thing to watch is the rehearsal. Watching the actors run through their lines during rehearsal can be worth while; this is where the scene blocking is taking place and where wardrobe gags might be developed, where actors might take off hats or coats, where unanticipated physical action could occur or where the director might want a piece of wardrobe for set dressing. After the rehearsal, the electricians and grips will take time to light and there will be time to prepare for anything that came out of the rehearsal. Many times the lighting gaffer will be able to tell you approximately how much time they plan on before they will be ready for a camera rehearsal. This is the time when the actors will go back to make-up, their trailers, or join the director for a line reading. This is also the last time for a little maintenance, before shooting.

The Designer. Here, there are no rules. The Designer has to be where the Designer has to be. Some mornings, especially the first morning of a costume change for an actor, the Designer will want to be making sure that the clothes fit properly, that accessories are there, that the hair and make-up people have any pertinent information and/or hair trimming pieces that are to be used.

When the cast is set, the Designer will want to oversee the dressing of the extra crowd, making sure that the background characters are as they want them; and as everything starts moving toward the set, the Designer will want to go there also, together with the Supervisor, whenever possible. It doesn't do much good to get to the set late and complain about the way things look.

Most directors and first assistants want the Designer on set in the morning, especially on days when a cast member is working in a new change. It's good politics also, making everyone comfortable with the fact that the department is represented on the set at the beginning of each day.

As Designer, I would always hand carry my favorite background jewelry or women's hats or any special pieces to the set rather than put them on extras in the morning. When getting to the set, I would query the set person about the action and blocking; then try and work with the second AD in placing background extras. I always felt that I could make a contribution here, because, I've just seen the extras getting dressed and know the better-looking "character" types. After placing the extras to camera and seeing where and what the shot was, I would then pass out the better pieces of costume jewelry and clothing that I wanted to be sure to get into the shot.

If the cast was new, then I'd be sure to show the director the new change. Most of the time, there had been so much communication about everything that everything was fine, but sometimes something would have changed, perhaps a replaced actor, and there would be a little last-minute scramble to get things right.

The Set Person starts matching the day's work — we always used to photograph the actors right **after** they established their changes, in front of camera with a Polaroid camera, and tape the photo into the script on the back of the page, across from the scene where the change worked. Now set people are photographing costume shots on the set with digital

167

cameras, then printing the photos out on computer, mounting the color photographs in clear plastic three-ring document holders for the set book. If you do it this way, be sure to note the scene number and "interior" or "exterior" on the photo, otherwise you'll have a big stack of photos with no way to relate them to a scene for matching.

Back at the truck. The Supervisor's department work day starts. Clean up after the extra fitting. Laundry out. Laundry back from the cleaners has to be hung, sized, and returned to stock. There are as many ways to organize stock as there are people doing it; but the main thing is to keep things together. There's nothing worse than finding something you want to use, buying or renting it, taking it on location with the desire to see it in a certain scene, and when that day comes — you can't find it and lose the opportunity; only to find, when doing returns at the end of the show, that the piece is hanging where it shouldn't be. As they used to tell me "If you can't find it, you might as well not have it."

We went over hanging outfits by type in Chapter 15 — it doesn't stop. No matter what system you choose, whatever quiet time you have can be spent "massaging" it. Putting everything in size order. Checking boxes to make sure that the contents are what you think. Checking the stock for hand "spotting" or cleaning, repairs, things you can use on up-coming characters.

Speaking of sizing clothes — we always screwed a yard stick down to the edge of a counter or used clear tape over a measuring tape for a size guide. Men's coats are sized under the arm hole with the coat laying flat on the yard stick. The trick to sizing is knowing how the garment is intended to fit, for example: a military jacket, which has to fit snugly, is measured seam to seam. A sport coat or suit coat, which has some play, is measured two inches down in size (about the length of your last thumb joint); this takes out about four inches. An overcoat might have four inches per side taken out, leaving room for a suit underneath.

Pants are measured by hooking up the front and placing the waistband on the yardstick — whatever it measures, double it; that's the waist size. The other measurement is the inseam; that's the distance along the seam, inside the pant leg from crotch to the bottom of the cuff.

A dress shirt is measured for: neck opening, button-to-button hole; and sleeve length, center back collar band to end of cuff.

Loose-fitting sport shirts can be measured across the chest and tagged with the inch measurement or **L, M, S.**

Women's clothes should always be sized by inches and not by dress sizes — 2, 3, 4, 5, 6, 7, 8, etc. These measurements are very undependable in that they have changed over the years and are not standard now, in many instances.

Once arriving at the size, it is written on a shipping tag, sometimes with a code for type of garment (example: a men's suit tag might read: S. B. 4-B 3pc., for, single-breasted, four-button closure at coat front, three piece with vest) because, once hung in stock, only the sleeve will be visible.

When tagging a garment always use a safety pin, which can be removed with out tearing, and pin the tag through the button hole at the cuff or to the inside lining; this will create a uniformity and lessen the damage to the sleeve material.

Hats, when pinned to outfits, should always be pinned through the inside hat band in the back. A pin through the hat brim will create holes and damage, and a pin through the front of the hat band will result in a rough spot that will hit an actor right on the forehead.

169

Every show prepares to the very end. There are always things that need work, or fittings for late-arriving cast, or getting ready for that next extra crowd, not to mention the paperwork and budget meetings; when you start to wind down, you can start the wrap.

The shooting day ends with everyone re-capturing the clothes. Extras are checked in, and costumes checked for missing items and cleaning. Cast clothing is returned to the truck, checked for cleaning and repairs.

The last thing is to go over the advance call sheet for the next shooting day and make sure that all is ready for the morning.

If everyone is on weekly time cards, you can keep a weekly hour calendar, recording report, lunch, and finish times for the week on a daily basis — shortening those Saturday night conversations that consist of questions like "What time did we go to lunch on Monday?"

Of course, every type of show has its own quirks, for instance, intensive stunt shows have their own unique requirements.

On shows where there's a car crash or some other lone stunt, the work of fitting, rigging, or dealing with safety equipment, can be done by the set crew; but action shows, Westerns, war dramas can be a separate challenge. If your show is going to be stunt intensive, you might consider a separate crew of one person or more to just take care of the stunt people.

A stunt person's first concern is safety, the second concern is working as quickly as possible. Wardrobe is not really important to them per se, it's just something that they have to deal with in order to get in front of the camera. Some common stunt items might include:

A cable rig of some kind, where a corset-like garment is worn. The corset has metal studs protruding, so that cables or wires can be attached, enabling the stunt man to "fly." After the costume is put on over the corset, holes have to be cut in the clothes to pass the cables through.

A "jerk-off" rig is similar to the cable rig. Used a lot in Westerns. A harness is worn on the upper body with a ring in the center back. After the coat is put on, a hole is cut in the back and the cable attached. The stunt person rides toward camera, reaches the end of the cable and is "jerked-off" the horse.

Stunt pads: worn by all stunt people in general, these consist of forearm, elbow, shin, knee and hip pads; hip pads are worn in an elastic waist girdle. These are common sports items and found at sporting goods stores. When worn they will take up extra room under any garment, necessitating larger waist sizes and sometimes larger sleeve or pant leg width.

Squibs: the most common device used on stunt people. Squibs are handled by the special effects crew. A "squib" is a small round metal dish fitted with a light explosive charge behind a prophylactic filled with stage blood. It is taped into clothing using heavy duty fabric tape; wires are then run from the explosive charge, down pant legs to an electric board. When the effects man makes contact on the board, the charge fires, blowing the stage blood through the clothing. To be sure that the charge gets through the fabric, the back of the clothing is sometimes "scored" with a razor blade. This usually leaves a large cross-shaped rip, about four inches by four inches, in the garment.

Any of these stunt rigs is hard on costumes. When possible, the set person should try and help the stunt team rig for a stunt where holes are going to be cut in clothing; with a little effort, sometimes, clothing seams can be opened instead of cutting holes in the body of the garment, helping to preserve the costume and save on later Loss and Damage.

Just a note on stage blood; If liquid soap is added to the blood, it will come out easier. Sometimes, someone will tell you that the blood is "washable," and sometimes it is, however, a little liquid soap won't change the look of the blood and is good insurance.

Story: *Rambo III* was an action picture that took me around the world. We shot for months; most of the time two units, sometimes three. At every location Rambo would engage in shoot-outs with the Russian army. We had dressed the rank and file Russian soldiers in camouflage jumpsuits, and on the big stunt days, would shoot the same 10 to 15 stunt men, over and over and over. The effects crew wanted 50 coveralls on their truck at all times, in order to pre-rig the insides with squibs. Fifty coveralls was a lot to me, since I sometimes had 50 extra soldiers dressed, plus the stunt team in multiples, which had to be cycled through a day's laundry and repair service.

The solution? We parked a small five-ton truck next to the effects truck. In the five-ton, we had a sewing machine and all the stunt clothing. Next to the truck, galvanized tubs filled with water, and between trucks we strung a clothesline.

171

We would hear the gunshots from the set. The bloody stunt crew would come to the wardrobe truck. We would undress them. They would use the water from one tub to wash up while we pulled the dead squib rigging out of their coveralls. We threw the squib rigging back into the effects truck for them to re-set, while the bloody coveralls were rinsed in another tub, then hung to dry. The stunt team then drew another, freshly rigged set of coveralls from the effects truck, and headed back to the set. The dry coveralls came off the clothesline and went to the sewing machine to be repaired, after which they would be given back to the effects crew to be pre-rigged for the next shot. This went on for weeks and weeks. By the time we were through shooting, the coveralls were a solid mass of zigzag repair lines. Why didn't we get more coveralls? In the beginning we had the simulated Russian camouflage material specially printed in the States at a commercial printer with a large minimum order; at this stage, we were shooting in Israel and our lines of communication made it difficult to engineer the project by phone. Besides, what we were doing was working and I had other things that I needed my budget for.

Speaking of foreign locations, my friend, Jo Korer, a Designer/Supervisor from England works in non-English-speaking countries all the time and has written the following:

Filming abroad in a non-English speaking country is not as simple as it may seem.

For this very reason I love it. I love the challenge, I love the surprises (of which there are always many!), I love the different cultures, I love seeing the faces of people watching in amazement as the department unfolds into something they could never have imagined was possible. I love every exciting, unpredictable moment that comes with the uniqueness of "Filming Away."

Filming away is most certainly not for everyone, and most certainly not for the timid or faint hearted. When, for example, you are asked by either the Costume Designer or a producer to supervise a department that will be filming away, it's usually because they hope you have that special skill required to work with people in their own country, culture, and all that may encompass.

Back in 1989 I flew out to Moscow to work on a movie called *The Russia House*, with Sean Connery and Michelle Pfeiffer. I was part of an historical event, because no Hollywood movie had ever shot in Russia before.

One of my first duties was to re-design a rather old, but still drivable, passenger coach into a costume truck. With my translator in tow I met the driver and then watched his face drop in absolute horror as it was translated to him that the first thing I was going to have to do was to take out all the seats, and drill rails into the ceiling, so that I could then hang the costumes. The concept of attaching a water tank to the undercarriage of his vehicle so that I could plumb in a washing machine, which I had brought with me from London, was far too much for him to comprehend. The washing machine never did get plumbed in! That beauty was eventually plumbed into my bathroom back at my hotel, and the tumble dryer into my bedroom. All, oh so glamorous!

But with firm, polite discussions over a bottle of Vodka, and the promise that passengers would indeed be sitting back in his red plastic seats, as if nothing had happened once the filming was over, seemed to put his mind at ease (they were worse for wear, to say the least, torn and dirty but, hey, they were red plastic after all!). He became very fond of our little costume set up and did, in fact, see how he could earn a better living from hiring out his truck as a costume vehicle to Russian movies rather than continue as a tour coach to tourists. The point of this story is to show how doing it the "Russian way" in a run-down bar, over a bottle of the best vanilla Vodka, won his trust.

Take time to investigate the country you are going to be working in, learn about their culture, ascertain what is polite and most certainly what is seen as impolite, thus encouraging mutual respect and trust. This is vital for any relationship to succeed.

Whilst I was working on a TV series recently in Hungary, for HBO called *John Adams*, I had an interesting meeting with the local unit manager. His job is to organize all the facilities for the production, i.e., tents, trailers, toilets etc. I explained and showed him a costume of the period which was nearly as wide as it was tall! I politely suggested a larger size "port-a-toilet" would be required. On the first day of shooting with our large call of extras, lo and behold the unit manager really had not taken on board just how important my request had been. There were 100 ladies, and not one of them could fit in the conveniences that had been provided. I immediately jumped on to this, and requested for the second time larger facilities but was told that there were no larger ones available in Hungary. I quickly retorted 'What about wheel chair access facilities?'. 'Oh we have those,' was the unit manager's reply.

Hey presto, larger facilities were soon available.

What is needed is Professionalism, Patience, Humility, Respect, Diplomacy, and Understanding.

I would like to really emphasize the word "patience" for all areas of working away in a non-English speaking country.

This brings to mind a scene from the movie *Lost In Translation*.

Anyone who has seen this wonderful film will know what I am talking about. For those who have not, please go and rent it, even if it's just to see the fantastic scene where Bill Murray is trying to shoot the whisky commercial for which he's been hired, and he tells his translator to ask the director one simple question… "does he want me to turn from the right or from the left ?"

A simple uncomplicated question that would normally get a quick simple uncomplicated answer, but no, not in the context of *Lost in Translation*, which the film so brilliantly depicts.

That one simple question Bill Murray asks starts a tirade of cross-fire, highly animated conversation between the translator and the director which is just pure genius. It is a situation I have, and still find myself in, on a daily basis when working away. Why? I have no idea. That is still a question, even after all these years, that I am still unable to answer.

Many times I would ask my translator, "Is there a problem?" A sharp reply of "No" comes back my way, and the tirade continues. How come my translator

173

could answer my question so quickly and easily? Yet any other question I may ask him to put to someone else seems to go on forever? This is a mystery I will take, unanswered, to my grave!

Working in Thailand was a wonderful experience. I love and totally respect the people, their culture, and their beliefs. They are a very polite, gentle race. The Thai culture is pure, and they never wish to disappoint. However this can, in itself, pose a problem to be resolved.

When working there it soon became apparent to me that they hated the words "I cannot." They would never say "no" to anything you asked them to do.

So, for instance, I would ask through the trusted translator to please tell a dresser or driver to go out and buy supplies. I would hand over a list, money and then think no more of it and go about my other duties. Before I knew it, maybe four or five hours had gone by, on a job that should have taken only an hour at the most. Upon their eventual return I would find out that they had been afraid to come back without the list being completed, having been unable to finish the task because one of the items was either out of stock or just not available.

It took me many weeks to prove to them that it was OK to clarify an uncertainty, that it was OK to not be able to fulfill the list, as long as they were truthful with me, thus giving me time to find an alternative solution.

Eventually, by showing them gentle, professional kindness they began to trust that I would not punish them, or be bitterly disappointed in them. Hopefully, I helped them to understand that they would not "lose face" because of being unable to find a pair of red cotton socks!

"Exhausting" is another word I would like to emphasize, not because of the long hours, but because if you find yourself working in a country where the culture may be one of bartering, with no department store or shop in sight then just a simple "nip out and buy" can turn into a major event. All you are trying to do is buy an item that is basic and simple, but the transaction is not.

Not forgetting that a big part of a Supervisor's job is to monitor and keep to the budget, it is in your own interest that your purchase is as cheap as possible, and this may include sitting crossed legged on a dusty market floor, faking sipping some awful smelling liquid that you have been assured is tea, while having to wear that big straw hat with bells and pompoms on it, being photographed holding a baby, with a whistle in your mouth, while the grandparents sit on your lap. And all to secure that cheap deal.

174

When working away in a non-English speaking country, you also have to be prepared to listen to your local team. Don't be so presumptuous to assume that you know everything – your local team can also be your greatest allies.

The one thing your local team will know about is their own country, with all the little idiosyncrasies that make that country the interesting place it is.

Always hold meetings with your crew and always communicate what is happening, thus encouraging teamwork. You will then be very pleasantly surprised as to how hearing their side of things can actually prove a great help to you.

Translation and Interpretation — two very different words — can make or break a team.

Different countries have different ways of constructing a sentence. For instance, in Germany they usually start their sentences with the words, "you will'" which could easily sound to the English like an order. In Serbia, they usually start a sentence with the word "listen," but when it is translated into English it may be misconstrued as a challenge when, in actual fact, it is just literally their interpretation of the translation. Be mindful of this at all times in all countries.

When working on a film, the majority of the film crew becomes very close and the actual department you are working in becomes even closer. They become your surrogate family, for better or for worse. A variety of personalities are thrown together so quickly, and into such a high-octane situation, it's astounding. Not only do you have to "get on" and do the job instantly, but you also have to start giving orders just as quickly to total strangers. This can cause a lot of resentment very quickly if it is not handled in an appropriate manner.

The fact that, in their eyes, a lot of foreign people have suddenly invaded not only their country, but also taken away their jobs, can cause resentment and jealousy.

Tread carefully, be mindful of this on every job and at all times. You want your co-workers to be happy and ensure that it's not too long before they realize why you are the "chosen one." Be a kind ear, always be available to listen, whether it be a personal or professional problem. Always be approachable and never make any of your crew feel that they cannot come to you.

I know Supervisors who have the attitude "don't bring your domestic problems to the work place" and, of course, to a certain extent that is correct, especially when time is money. And never has that saying been truer than when working on a film. But, if it's affecting the work performance then it should not be ignored and you should at least show genuine concern, and see if you can help.

This situation is even more important when working away, as so many of the countries that are chosen for filming are selected because it is cheaper to work there than in the US or the UK. What you have to be prepared for is that the very people who live in these countries will have problems that you, or I, can never imagine having to deal with. Their lifestyle may be very different to what we are used to in the West.

Juggling all the above is not easy. Some say you can learn it, but I still believe it is an innate part of who you are. If you're a person who genuinely likes people, enjoys solving problems, thinking literally "on your feet," loves film, then this is the job for you.

I hope this gives you as much pleasure reading it, as it has given me living it.

★The best thing I ever learned on location — using a bed sheet to carry clothes instead of hangers. Sometimes the ground makes rolling racks impossible — fold set costumes onto a sheet, tie the corners, and carry the bundle to the set — works great.

BACK C
940-

oor guys
going up
hill
CLEANEST
(SOME
NEW
GUYS)

OKINAWA
STAGE 2 of 3
911 -
MOVING UP

WET·HUMID-

- WOOL SHIRTS
& M-41 JACKETS
OK

- VERY DIRTY

SCN#
915

177

SCN#915 PANTS OUT OVER
LEGGINGS OK

PANitte

Marine on Okinawa

OKINAWA
- ARMY TROOPS - '383 RD'

STENCIL
CAMO NET,-
'TAN WIGGLE'
CAMO BANDS

SOFT CAPS UNDER HELMET

DARK GREEN WEBBING

27TH. DIV

L 'BYTE' UNIT PATCH
(SOME CHEVRONS)

SOME M-41'S
SOME TAN PONCHOS

OVERALL DIRTY
SOME
'WALKING
WOUNDED'

L M44 BOOTS

SAME
AS SOLDIERS
GUARDING JAPANESE
PRISONERS

P. Motte

Army Soldier on Okinawa

chapter **19**

TELEVISION

Most of this book is applicable to both feature films and television but, television does have its own peculiarities, so we should take a look at them.

The big difference between most film projects and TV is time and scale (which means budget). Features come in all sizes, but many will average two to three months of preparation time and sometimes more, and shoot on a schedule of one to two pages per day, meaning that a script of 120 pages will shoot over a 60- to 72-day schedule, sometimes five, sometimes six days per week, or something like three months. Also, the finished product will be conceived to be displayed on a screen that might average 20 feet tall. Therefore, things have to be truly "picture perfect," because a shirt collar might be 10 feet tall; but once you get into a set or sequence, you usually will have some time before the next set works, and that time is additional preparation time.

Television comes in five basic shapes: commercials (including in-fomercials), music videos, movies-of-the-week (MOWs), mini-series and series. Industrials made for industry training are long-form infomercials.

If there is one big difference in features and television, it is the final size of the product — although, today, with the large plasma screens available, that's less so. In the old days, it was always tempting to think that you could get away with more cheating on television because the smaller screen size meant things wouldn't be seen as much. By the time you see people full-figure, they are only a few inches tall; and there tend to be **lots** of close-ups in TV, so you really had to pay attention to the area around the face, letting the rest fall off, if necessary. This is true — but it's good to never bring this into your thinking, because there's nothing more hated by producers than hearing someone say "It doesn't matter, it's only TV." Also, remember, while the finished product will be smaller than the **Big Screen** — all your fittings with actors in front of directors and producers will be full size, and sometimes that's more important than what will be seen later, because all people like to think that they're getting product that's "feature quality."

The skill is to give everyone a "feature look" on a TV budget.

The following is from Loree Parral. Loree is a working Supervisor who's been nominated several times during the past 30 years for Emmys (winning two) for costumes. She's also had several write-ups in magazines for her trend-setting costuming of stars on her shows:

"Costuming for episodic television is like running a relay race every seven to eight days. You are primed and ready and waiting for the baton to be handed off and then it's on you! You must distill input and multiple visions from producers, directors, writers, a cinematographer, sound mixer, production designer and yes, actors, into one coherent definition of a character via wardrobe — all with limited time and money.

It is also an endurance test to be able to keep the pace up for 10 months: script after script, week in and week out, 14-hour day after 14-hour day. For me, the most gratifying aspect of the job has been when all the players in this very collaborative enterprise were happy with the end result and only I knew how utterly impossible the task seemed at the onset!

The job itself is not unlike costuming for a feature, movie-of-the-week or a commercial. There is a script, concepts, meetings, casting, budgeting, scheduling, clothing procurement, fittings, shoot and wrap. The primary difference is that in episodic television, you are doing more than one script simultaneously. You are shooting one episode (or as is becoming more common, two episodes), while prepping one or two more and wrapping yet another, all at the same time. You may have two to five scripts 'in your head' at a time.

Staying organized and keeping precise records of all the elements for each episode is the key to staying sane in episodic TV. Every costumer should create a system that will provide a means of tracking all the pertinent data, e.g., costume changes, petty cash expenditures, purchase order logs and itemizations. There are several software programs available for aiding in all this paper chase. I have found that most costumers have modified existing tools or created their own to provide an individualized approach with which they feel most comfortable. For example, after 30 years, I still use my system of keeping cast information on 5 x 8 index cards: it's easy to update, portable, and inexpensive to maintain.

The other element that is crucial for a successful and happy experience is the cooperation and cohesiveness of the entire wardrobe crew. Open and frequent communication with the other costumers is critical. Because the pace of television can be hectic, important information can be lost if not verbally communicated, as well as reflected on the plot sheets and tags accompanying each costume.

No one person or job works alone; it is truly a team effort. Support as well as respect for everyone's role in the process must also extend to the other departments on the production. A cooperative relationship with the art department, camera, props, sound, make-up and hair cannot be emphasized enough. It is simply an avenue to a more enjoyable and productive experience for everyone."

181

An outline of the various types of television productions follows:

COMMERCIALS / INFOMERCIALS:

Most of these are "modern day" and feature a product with a host, but some can be production heavy and period. The client usually (sometimes through advertising firms) contracts the work through independent production houses that are set up to do these and have track records. Preparation time can be short and usually done under the, sometimes partial, supervision of the agency art director. There are a lot of vested interests on these shoots: clients, advertising agencies, and in-house directors. Work can be found at the agency and production-house level and many successful commercial stylists have formed professional relationships with sought-after directors. These folks work a lot and more than one have become Costume Designers on features when their directors graduated to that arena.

MUSIC VIDEOS:

These can be the most difficult and the most rewarding. Difficult, because there are so many and everyone is reaching for something different — fresh; hot; and because there may be a lot of people (musicians, artists, producers, friends, production folks), who will want to have their ideas realized. Many of these shoots are highly conceptualized and call for heavy shopping and/or costume construction. I think that here is where you either need to be a quick sketch artist or have a good one handy. The ability to direct the process by offering quick paper concepts that many people can agree on can get you started quickly. Traditionally, this is the area of the hip-shopper who can get choices into meetings and fittings on a short schedule. There isn't a budget format here because sometimes a little, sometimes a lot of money will be available — but all the rules of breakdown and schedule apply. Always get complete real measurements (by tape measure) of all the talent before shopping.

The shape of the department will depend on where the shooting will take place and how clothing-intensive it is.

182

MOVIES-OF-THE-WEEK:

Really these are small features. Typically they prep for four to six weeks and shoot for five weeks or 25 to 30 days. That's an average of four to five pages per day. Large sequences are sometimes shot in a day or two, instead of a week, as on a feature, so the prep time is less between sequences, and the costumes are turned around faster. The saving grace is that MOWs are about actors saying lines — so, usually, as long as the people directly on camera are acceptable, you're covered, because the background isn't as critical, it just isn't seen as much because of the screen size.

MINI-SERIES:

Long-form television. These are usually big budget, big production value efforts — think: *Band of Brothers*, *Pacific*, *Winds of War*, *Rome*, etc. These are monsters. Lots of actors, usually with many costume changes, tons of extras, trucks full of clothes with a shooting schedule of six months or more. Sometimes one director, sometimes two different directors who leap-frog episodes, sometimes shooting simultaneously, often with second units. These take large staffs with plenty of experience at the top. The wardrobe department can look like this: Designer and Design Assistants, show Supervisor, shoppers, PAs, office personnel, in-house driver(s), workroom, warehouse and fitting crew, aging and dyeing shop, specialty manufacture person(s), Set Supervisor, set crew(s), cleaning/laundry crew(nights). These shows usually have to have large base camps to house the department and dress extras and, when they change locations, the move is major. Organization is everything.

SERIES:

Usually there is a "pilot" shot first. These shows run a half hour or an hour. Usually, an hour show is shot in six days — averaging 60 pages to an hour that equates to 10 pages shot per day — that's fast. Many of these shows are shot at a studio with many "home" sets built on stages; that means that the day consists of shooting scenes and moving between standing sets. Actors will have costume changes during the day, sometimes in the same set for different scenes. Many times the shows are geared to exterior location shooting (police dramas) which might call for a few days on stage and a few days out on local locations. On these shows, there is usually a hard wall department with office, stock area, fitting rooms and tailor shop, and a trailer which is loaded each night with the clothes for the next day. The trailer is then moved to the stage or daily location, as needed. These shows have sometimes large regular casts. Each cast member has to have a defined personality and will have many changes, necessitating a large standing closet for each character, which may change each season to reflect current fashion styles. There also will be a regular influx of guest actors who play central roles in each episode — they are sometimes cast last minute, maybe the night before they work — this means late-night shopping and alterations.

On series there will be many directors who will like to put their stamps where they can, but the shows are set to a longer, producer's vision and network agreement, so the ground rules will be laid down early as to what's acceptable. But, as all involved get comfortable with the idea that they will work for years at 12 to 15 shows per season, peoples' minds will change on "whom" they are and what they want to wear.

Because of the nature of this format, once rolling, it feels like a steady job, a day-to-day existence based on shooting script material that comes in less than a week ahead. The routine becomes: quick preparation; detailed breakdowns; a good alterations shop; and friendly relations with producers and unit manager (line producer). Changes are to be expected.

Liana
Concept for TV pilot, *Legend of Liana*

Concept art for TV pilot
Lessons Learned

chapter **20**

THE WRAP

As the end of shooting moves closer, you get closer to the last big job; the return of all the rented costumes and the disposition of all purchases.

You will have only two types of inventory in the department; "yours" and "theirs."

I have been on shows that had ample wrap time and shows that wanted everyone off the clock the day after shooting; but no matter how much or how little time you have, the job of wrapping the department stays the same.

Wrap time should have been figured into your first budget and discussed with the line producer from the beginning, taking the following into consideration: 1) What's the last thing we shoot? Often times, the show will finish with stage work, pick-up shots or other small scenes. If this is the case, then the last weeks or days of shooting can be used as wrap time. Whatever isn't working can be cleaned, mended, sorted, and packed. If, however, the last days of shooting are large scale, and your crew is engaged in handling the set, then that same amount of labor effort for cleaning, sorting, mending, and packing, will have to be done after the company wraps in the week(s) following production; 2) How much will it cost? The biggest expense after shooting will be dealing with the rental houses' charges for what **they** have to do to get your clothes back into their stock. If you don't sort things out because your labor is cut off, then the costume house will have to sort things out at **their** labor cost. If you don't clean and mend your rented clothes, then the costume house will clean and mend at **their** labor cost. If you have rented items that are missing or damaged and don't make an effort to replace them with items that you (your company) owns, then you will be billed for the **full replacement price**. In some cases, in-house tailor-made prices or **10 times the amount of the rental**. It's good to remember that when you rent anything, you are **borrowing** someone else's things for a price; those folks (businesses) have a right to expect that you treat **their** things with professional respect, and if you don't, you have the right to expect that they will charge you for it.

The way to minimize Loss and Damage charges when returning rented costumes is simple; return things in the condition in which you took them out.

The ideal wrap would go something like this: After shooting has finished, all costumes would be sent out, cleaned, and returned to the department. (Although sometimes this won't work. If your location is somewhere where there is no cleaners, or the small-town cleaners can't remove the blood, aging or make-up in your clothes, the costume rental house will have to clean them again, anyway. Also, remember, if you clean the clothes, pack them, and ship them back to their points of origin, and they arrive crumpled, from being packed, and are unsuitable for rehanging in costume house stock, the costume house will have to send them out again for a steam and press. You might want to check with the rental house first, to come to some kind of understanding on this.)

The costumes are then checked for repairs and any damages to the clothes are corrected. This usually entails a sewing machine and hand repair, but when the rental house accepts its clothes back, they are always checked for ill-use and billed accordingly. So, mending garments, cleaning and stuffing shoes, steaming hats, while a bit labor- and time-consuming, pays off against L/D charges.

The clothes would then be sorted by costume house. Most houses stamp their names inside the garments; sometimes the stamps look the same. Most (but not all) rental houses will refuse items returned to them that are stamped from another costume house. This will cause you problems if, at the end of your shoot, you return things to three or so places. One or two might call you later and tell you that you have losses with them, and further, some of the returned clothes are not theirs. That requires you to make another round and try to get the right pieces to the right places. Some places use bar-code stickers, but the process is the same.

188

Once separated by costume house, the clothes are then assembled according to billing sheet; this is made harder with computer sheets — a lot of costumers are demanding itemized sheets, as well as computer-inventory billing. If you have rented according to group — cowboys/Indians, etc. — the assembly is easier. The items are then tagged with the sheet and line number corresponding to billing sheet. This way, the show's rentals are being assembled in reverse and when you're finished, you will know, ahead of time, where your losses are. This will allow you to make preparations to construct, purchase or somehow substitute for, or pay for, them. This works to the advantage of your company because it allows con-sideration of options in advance, eliminating being blindsided by late and unexpected bills for Loss and Damage from a forgotten vendor.

Now your show can be packed for shipment home. Sometimes I've used TV boxes, filling each one with items from one sheet and writing the sheet number on top; sometimes the clothes are returned in a truck or "E" containers, either way, if they are returned according to sheet number, the shipping department at the rental house can check in your show more quickly with less labor, and your final billing will be completed faster.

Finally, items that your show owns, which you want to trade for Loss and Damage, should be handled separately and dealt with last, face to face, based on what the rental house knows about the losses and damages.

On a little Viet Nam show, we wrapped about three o'clock, on a Thursday morning in the rain, with heaps of wet and muddy clothes, heaps of wet and muddy costumers. The unit manager wanted us to throw everything in boxes and leave the island location by Saturday… Sunday at the latest.

Our discussion followed familiar lines; we had to clean everything, sort everything, dry everything, separate and mend everything, then pack everything for shipment. Okay — could we take Sunday off and have everything ready to ship by next Wednesday? Yes, we would try.

We came in later Friday and got out the cleaning. Saturday we cleaned muddy boots. Monday we started repairing the cleaning and packing what we could. The way things were spread out, we weren't going to get an inventory; the UPM said he didn't care, we would have to figure it out back in town.

Tuesday everything got packed. We were told that everything was to be shipped by barge and would take a week to get back to Los Angeles. We told the UPM that this would result in the clothes, boots especially, getting mildewed. That would have to be another thing that would be sorted out in L.A., so Wednesday the boxes were put in a container for shipment.

As luck would have it, we and the container met in L.A., the week of Thanksgiving. The UPM didn't want to pay us for the holiday and so we were told to start the unpacking and wrap after another week, and that we would have only a week to wrap — make all the returns to four costume houses, etc.

When we came back to those boxes and unpacked them, there were over two hundred pair of very mildewed boots. There was no way that the two of us could clean these boots and do the rest of the return... so, we had to hire two additional people for a week to clean the boots. We had to send out much of the hanging stock to the cleaners for the same reason.

When the returns were complete, we were presented with a bill from one costume house for over $16,000 in Loss and Damage, for missing items. We were astounded. In checking the bill we found that the policy of this house was to charge 10 times the amount of the rental for losses. On the bottom of most rental contracts there's a stipulation that they **can** charge up to 10 times the rental price, but most houses charge a reasonable amount, based on whether the missing items are easily obtainable or not. In this case, war surplus should be charged at the purchase price, plus a house fee of 20% to 35%. A pair of boots that retail for $25 might cost $35. We were being charged $250 per pair, based on a $25 rental.

I spent another week on payroll rounding up missing pieces. I spent about $1,200 and satisfied $16,000 in Loss and Damage charges.

The problems stay the same — only the people change.

Pocahontas in English dress

Native Warrior study

chapter **21**

REFERENCE

The following chapter contains names and addresses of costume houses, an assortment of sketches, samples of breakdown forms previously discussed.

The following list is in no particular order, and is (of course) only a partial list of costume houses, worldwide.

COSTUME RENTAL HOUSES IN THE UNITED STATES:

Bill Hargate Costumes
Phone: (213) 876-4432
1111 N. Formosa
Los Angeles, CA 90046

Costume Rental Corp.
Phone: (818) 753-3700
11149 Vanowen St.
North Hollywood, CA 91605

Motion Picture Costume Co.
Phone: (818) 764-8191
6844 Lankershim Blvd.
North Hollywood, CA 91605

Palace Costume Co.
Phone: (213) 651-5458
835 North Fairfax Ave.
Los Angeles, CA 90046

Local # 705, Motion Picture Costumers
Phone: (818) 487-5655
4731 Laurel Canyon, Suite # 201
Valley Village, Ca. 91607
motionpicturecostumers705.org

Local # 892, Costume Designers Guild
Phone: (818) 752-2400
11969 Venture, First floor
Studio City, Ca. 91604
costumedesignersguild.com

Repeat Performance
Phone: (213) 938-0609
318 North La Brea Ave.
Los Angeles, CA 90036

The Helen Larson Collection
Phone: (818) 760-0900
(This fabulous collection of vintage clothing was sold to Western Costume)

Eastern Costume Company
Phone: (818) 982-3611
7243 Coldwater Canyon
North Hollywood, CA 91605

United-American Costumes
Phone: (818) 764-2239
12980 Raymer St.
North Hollywood, CA 91605

Western Costume Co.
Phone: (818) 760-0900
11041 Vanowen St.
North Hollywood, CA 91605
(A Hollywood legend – they have something of everything)

Silvia's Costumes
Phone: (323) 666-0680
4964 Hollywood Blvd.
Los Angeles, CA 90027
(*silviascostumes.com*)
(Silvia's is unique in that they will custom print fabric and make samples).

Global Effects
Phone: (818) 503-9273
(They specialize in Sci-fi/fantasy)

Of course, there are *many* more costume places in Los Angeles, including all the major studio wardrobe departments, which you can find in source books like *Debbies*, listed below.

LEADING COSTUME HOUSES IN ENGLAND:
Academy Costumes Limited
Phone: (0) 20 7620 0771
50 Rushworth Street
London, SEI 0RB

Angels Costumes
Phone: (0) 20 8202 2244
1 Garrick Road, Hendon,
London, NW9 6AA

CosProp
Phone: (0) 20 7561 7300
469-475 Holloway Road,
London, N7 6 LE

Carlo Manzi Rentals
Phone: (0) 20 7625 6391
31-33 Liddell Road
London NW6 2EW

LEADING COSTUME HOUSES IN ITALY:
Peruzzi/Costumi d'Arte
Phone: 06-511-5928
Piazzale A Tosti, #4
00147 Roma, Italy

Pompeii
Phone: 39-6-487-4215
Via di S. Saba
5.00153 Roma, Italy

Tirelli Costumi
Phone: 39-6-321-2654
Via Pompeo Magno 11/B
00192 Roma Italy

LEADING COSTUME HOUSE IN AUSTRIA:
196
Lambert Hofer
Phone: 43-1-922-120
1150 Wien – 15, Hackengasse 10

LEADING COSTUME HOUSE IN SPAIN:
Casa Cornejo
Phone: 34-91-375-7290
Madrid Spain

For printed research, the *L.A. 411 Directory* and the *N.Y. 411 Directory* are hard to beat. They are a little expensive, but worth it. Also, *Debbies Book* is another source book that is full of information and businesses (*www.debbiesbook.com*), and at around $20.00, is a real bargain.

Following are some size conversion charts that may come in handy:

HATS: Measure in inches around the head. Military dress hats fit high on the head and are slightly smaller than civilian wear.

Hat Size	Hat Size	Inches	Distribution
XXS	6 3/8	20 to 20 1/8	1%
	6 1/2	20 1/4 to 20 1/2	
XS	6 5/8	20 3/4 to 21	4%
	6 3/4	21 1/8 to 21 3/8	
S	6 7/8	21 1/2 to 21 3/4	30%
	7	21 7/8 to 22 1/8	
M	7 1/8	22 1/4 to 22 1/2	44%
	7 1/4	22 5/8 to 22 7/8	
L	7 3/8	23 to 23 1/4	18%
	7 1/2	23 3/8 to 23 5/8	
XL	7 5/8	23 3/4 to 24	2.5%
	7 3/4	24 1/8 to 24 3/8	
XXL	7 7/8	24 1/2 to 24 3/4	.5%
	8	24 7/8 to 25 1/8	

GLOVES: To measure, put a measuring tape around the hand at the widest part not including the thumb.

Size	Size	Inches	Military Size
S	7 to 8	6 1/2 to 7	3
M	8 1/2 to 9 1/2	7 1/2 to 8	4
L	10 to 10 1/2	8 1/2 to 9	5
XL	11	9 5 to 10	–

BOOTS AND SHOES: from Men's sizes to Women's sizes, just take two sizes off the man's size. A man's 10 is a woman's 8.

INTERNATIONAL BOOT AND SHOE CONVERSATION CHART:

American	6	7	8	9	10	11	12
British	5	6	7	8.5	9	10	11
European	39	40	41	42	43	44	45
Asian	24.5	25	26	27	28	29	30

MEN'S APPAREL:
Suits (Normal 6" drop from chest to waist – Athletic cut is 8")

Chest	36	40	42	44	46	48	50
Waist	30	34	36	38	40	42	44
Size	S=34/36	M=38-40	L=42-44	XL=46-48	XXL=50	XXXL=52	

MEN'S SHIRTS:

Neck	13-13.5	14-14.5	15-15.5	16-16.5	17-17.5	18-18.5	19-19.5
	XS	S	M	L	XL	XXL	XXXL

WOMEN'S APPAREL:

Size	Bust	Waist	Hip	
2	32	23	34	
4	33	24	35	XS
6	34	25	36	
8	35	26	37	S
10	36	27	38	
12	37.5	28.5	39.5	M
14	39	30	41	
16	40.5	31.5	42.5	L
18	42	33	44	
20	44	35	46	XL
22H	48	39	50	XXL
24H	50	41	52	
26H	52	43	54	
28H	54	45	56	

ABOUT THE AUTHOR

RICHARD LA MOTTE was born in 1943 in Los Angeles to unknown parents. It is thought that his natural birth father was killed in WW2 and his birth mother put him up for adoption.

Richard was adopted in 1943 by Lucy and Ross La Motte, both naturalized American citizens: Ross, a Canadian WW1 veteran and Lucy, a child refugee from the Mexican revolution.

Raised in West Los Angeles, he graduated from University High School in winter 1961, an Art Major and promptly joined the United states Marine Corps, where he served for four years, 1961 – 1965. He assisted Intelligence and held a "Secret" clearance. He was awarded: three letters of commendation, a Good Conduct medal, and National Defense medal. He was separated in 1965 with an Honorable Discharge.

1965 – 1966 he worked as an Illustrator for Pacific Screen Co., a silkscreen company.

In 1966, he entered the Motion Picture Industry as a Stock Clerk at Fox Studio Wardrobe Department.

He worked as a Set Costumer on: *Batman, Brackens World, Voyage to the Bottom of the Sea, Lost in Space, Time Tunnel, M.A.S.H., Butch Cassidy and the Sundance Kid, Tora-Tora-Tora, Planet of the Apes, Hello Dolly, Doctor Dolittle, Little Big Man, Dillinger,* and many movies-of-the-week and TV pilots.

He was then drafted as Costume Designer for *The Wind and the Lion* and went on to do: *Goonies, Rambo III, The Return of a Man Called Horse, The Island of Doctor Moreau, Crazy Horse, Geronimo, Tecumseh, Broken Chain, Army of One, Hanoi Hilton, Hawken, Stitches, Gods and Generals,* and others.

From 1980 to 1984 he owned and operated Springboard Studios, one of L.A.'s first boutique studio sound stages and Cloud Dancer Productions, an "off-the-lot Art Department," specializing in costume, property and set design, and construction.

Working in independent films he directed *Hustle U* (TV release), produced/directed/production designed low-budget pilots at Springboard Studios. (*Legend of Liana, Police Shootings, The Art of Clowning, Imagination Library*, and others)

Richard has written several screenplays, optioning four.

1980 to 1990, Richard worked as production designer on many commercials and music videos and was represented by Storyboard, Inc., as a storyboard artist.

Richard has worked for: Western Costume Company, Eastern Costume Company, American Costume Company and Motion Picture Costume Company, in capacities ranging from stock person, to in-house designer.

Richard worked as technical advisor on: *Last of the Mohicans, Pacific*, and *Pearl Harbor* and is an industry-recognized expert on ethnic, period, and military costumes.

201

Retired in 2006 with 40 years motion picture experience, Richard joined his wife of 40 years, Patricia, in her real estate practice, while continuing to work as technical advisor, costume consultant, sketch artist, author, and guest speaker.

Since 2006, Richard has gained a California Real Estate License and certification in Home Staging, Short Sales and Foreclosure Sales and has gone back to school studying interior design.

Favorite subjects include: ancient history, comparative religion, metaphysics, new physics, economics, politics, art, native American cultures, construction of all types, health and consciousness.

Additional Education: Film School – Art Center, Pasadena California; Painting – Los Angeles Art Academy, Los Angeles; Interior Design – College of the Canyons, Santa Clarita California. Writing and Producing – U.C.L.A./ U.S.C. extension classes.

Online resume and gallery of art examples can be found at: *www. richardlamotte.com*

MASTER SHOTS
100 ADVANCED CAMERA TECHNIQUES TO GET AN EXPENSIVE LOOK ON YOUR LOW BUDGET MOVIE

CHRISTOPHER KENWORTHY

Master Shots gives filmmakers the techniques they need to execute complex, original shots on any budget. By using powerful master shots and well-executed moves, directors can develop a strong style and stand out from the crowd. Most low-budget movies look low-budget, because the director is forced to compromise at the last minute. *Master Shots* gives you so many powerful techniques that you'll be able to respond, even under pressure, and create knock-out shots. Even when the clock is ticking and the light is fading, the techniques in this book can rescue your film, and make every shot look like it cost a fortune.

Each technique is illustrated with samples from great feature films and computer-generated diagrams for absolute clarity.

Use the secrets of the master directors to give your film the look and feel of a multi-million-dollar movie. The set-ups, moves and methods of the greats are there for the taking, whatever your budget.

"Master Shots gives every filmmaker out there the blow-by-blow setup required to pull off even the most difficult of setups found from indies to the big Hollywood blockbusters. It's like getting all of the magician's tricks in one book."
— Devin Watson, Producer, *The Cursed*

"Though one needs to choose any addition to a film book library carefully, what with the current plethora of volumes on cinema, Master Shots *is an essential addition to any worthwhile collection."*
— Scott Essman, Publisher, *Directed By* Magazine

"Christopher Kenworthy's book gives you a basic, no holds barred, no shot forgotten look at how films are made from the camera point of view. For anyone with a desire to understand how film is constructed — this book is for you."
— Matthew Terry, Screenwriter/Director, Columnist
www.hollywoodlitsales.com

Since 2000, CHRISTOPHER KENWORTHY has written, produced, and directed drama and comedy programs, along with many hours of commercial video, tv pilots, music videos, experimental projects, and short films. He's also produced and directed over 300 visual FX shots. In 2006 he directed the web-based Australian UFO Wave, which attracted many millions of viewers. Upcoming films for Kenworthy include *The Sickness* (2009) and *Glimpse* (2011).

$24.95 · 240 PAGES · ORDER NUMBER 91RLS · ISBN: 9781932907513

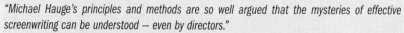

CINEMATIC STORYTELLING
THE 100 MOST POWERFUL FILM CONVENTIONS
EVERY FILMMAKER MUST KNOW

JENNIFER VAN SIJLL

BEST SELLER

How do directors use screen direction to suggest conflict? How do screenwriters exploit film space to show change? How does editing style determine emotional response?

Many first-time writers and directors do not ask these questions. They forego the huge creative resource of the film medium, defaulting to dialog to tell their screen story. Yet most movies are carried by sound and picture. The industry's most successful writers and directors have mastered the cinematic conventions specific to the medium. They have harnessed non-dialog techniques to create some of the most cinematic moments in movie history.

This book is intended to help writers and directors more fully exploit the medium's inherent storytelling devices. It contains 100 non-dialog techniques that have been used by the industry's top writers and directors. From *Metropolis* and *Citizen Kane* to *Dead Man* and *Kill Bill*, the book illustrates – through 500 frame grabs and 75 script excerpts – how the inherent storytelling devices specific to film were exploited.

You will learn:
· How non-dialog film techniques can advance story.
· How master screenwriters exploit cinematic conventions to create powerful scenarios.

"Cinematic Storytelling scores a direct hit in terms of concise information and perfectly chosen visuals, and it also searches out... and finds... an emotional core that many books of this nature either miss or are afraid of."
— Kirsten Sheridan, Director, *Disco Pigs*; Co-writer, *In America*

"Here is a uniquely fresh, accessible, and truly original contribution to the field. Jennifer van Sijll takes her readers in a wholly new direction, integrating aspects of screenwriting with all the film crafts in a way I've never before seen. It is essential reading not only for screenwriters but also for filmmakers of every stripe."
— Prof. Richard Walter, UCLA Screenwriting Chairman

JENNIFER VAN SIJLL has taught film production, film history, and screenwriting. She is currently on the faculty at San Francisco State's Department of Cinema.

$24.95 · 230 PAGES · ORDER NUMBER 35RLS · ISBN: 9781932907056

SETTING UP YOUR SHOTS, SECOND EDITION

GREAT CAMERA MOVES EVERY FILMMAKER SHOULD KNOW

JEREMY VINEYARD

This is the 2nd edition of one of the most successful filmmaking books in history, with sales of over 50,000 copies. Using examples from over 300 popular films, Vineyard provides detailed examples of more than 150 camera setups, angles, and moves which every filmmaker must know — presented in an easy-to-use "wide screen format." This book is the "Swiss Army Knife" that belongs in every filmmakers tool kit.

This new and revised 2nd edition of *Setting Up Your Shots* references over 200 new films and 25 additional filmmaking techniques.

This book gives the filmmaker a quick and easy "shot list" that he or she can use on the set to communicate with their crew.

The Shot List includes: Whip Pan, Reverse, Tilt, Helicopter Shot, Rack Focus, and much more.

"This is a film school in its own right and a valuable and worthy contribution to every filmmaker's shelf. Well done, Vineyard and Cruz!"
— Darrelyn Gunzburg, "For The Love Of It" Panel, *www.ForTheLoveOfIt.com*

"Perfect for any film enthusiast looking for the secrets behind creating film... It is a great addition to any collection for students and film pros alike....." Because of its simplicity of design and straight forward storyboards, this book is destined to be mandatory reading at films schools throughout the world."
— Ross Otterman, *Directed By* Magazine

"Setting Up Your Shots is a great book for defining the shots of today. The storyboard examples on every page make it an valuable reference book for directors and DP's alike! Great learning tool. Should be a boon for writers who want to choose the most effective shot and clearly show it in their boards for the maximum impact."
— Paul Clatworthy, Creator, StoryBoard Artist and StoryBoard Quick Software

JEREMY VINEYARD is currently developing an independent feature entitled "Concrete Road" with Keith David (*The Thing, Platoon*) and is working on his first novel, a modern epic.

$22.95 · 160 PAGES · ORDER NUMBER 84RLS · ISBN: 9781932907421

{ THE MYTH OF MWP }

In a dark time, a light bringer came along, leading the curious and the frustrated to clarity and empowerment. It took the well-guarded secrets out of the hands of the few and made them available to all. It spread a spirit of openness and creative freedom, and built a storehouse of knowledge dedicated to the betterment of the arts.

The essence of the Michael Wiese Productions (MWP) is empowering people who have the burning desire to express themselves creatively. We help them realize their dreams by putting the tools in their hands. We demystify the sometimes secretive worlds of screenwriting, directing, acting, producing, film financing, and other media crafts.

By doing so, we hope to bring forth a realization of 'conscious media' which we define as being positively charged, emphasizing hope and affirming positive values like trust, cooperation, self-empowerment, freedom, and love. Grounded in the deep roots of myth, it aims to be healing both for those who make the art and those who encounter it. It hopes to be transformative for people, opening doors to new possibilities and pulling back veils to reveal hidden worlds.

MWP has built a storehouse of knowledge unequaled in the world, for no other publisher has so many titles on the media arts. Please visit www.mwp.com where you will find many free resources and a 25% discount on our books. Sign up and become part of the wider creative community!

Onward and upward,

Michael Wiese
Publisher/Filmmaker